Study Guide to accompany

DOLLARS AND SENSE
An Introduction to Economics

Study Guide to accompany

DOLLARS AND SENSE
An Introduction to Economics

Prepared to accompany
the text by
Marilu Hurt McCarty

Third Edition

Eleanor D. Craig
University of Delaware

Scott, Foresman and Company

Glenview, Illinois

Dallas, Tex.
Oakland, N.J.
Palo Alto, Cal.
Tucker, Ga.
London, England

Prepared by

Eleanor D. Craig
University of Delaware

for

P.S. Associates
Sterling, Massachusetts

ISBN: 0-673-15604-4

TO THE STUDENT

The purpose of this *Study Guide to Accompany Dollars and Sense* is to help you learn and understand the subject matter of economics. It is not a substitute for the textbook or for classwork, but rather an important accompaniment to the text and to class. It provides a convenient guide for review, a means to sharpen your ability to use economic concepts, and a way to apply some of the theoretical material to real-world problems and current events.

Each of the chapters in the Study Guide parallels a chapter in the text. To assist you in learning the material, the format includes five means of review: a chapter summary, a set of twenty completion questions to help you organize the material in each chapter, a number of self-evaluation exercises and application questions, ten true/false questions, and twenty multiple-choice questions.

As you study the *Dollars and Sense* text and this Study Guide:

1. Read the text chapter rapidly, trying to get a feeling for the kind of material covered and for the direction that the chapter is taking.
2. Reread the chapter carefully, being certain to take the Self-Check quiz of multiple-choice questions and to review the Terms to Remember.
3. Work through the corresponding chapters in the Study Guide. Check your answers. Review the textbook material for those questions that you answered incorrectly.
4. Study the Topics for Discussion in the text at the back of each chapter and be able to address each of these topics.
5. Use the questions in the text and Study Guide to help review for quizzes and examinations.

Each chapter of the Study Guide contains:

I. Capsule Summary
    This section provides a summary and outline of the material in the chapter. This summary indicates the key concepts and sketches the general coverage and organization of the text chapter.

II. Reviewing the Chapter
    This section follows the text presentation very closely. Page references to the textbook material are given following each question. Most of the questions ask you to provide the missing word or phrase. Some sentence completion exercises offer several alternative words or phrases to choose from. Answers to the questions in this section are given at the end of each chapter. If you answers are different from those given in the answer key, refer back to the text for further study on the pages listed.

III. Self-Evaluation Exercises and Applications
    This section applies the theory learned in the chapter to current topics by requiring you to work examples and draw graphs or charts to illustrate the more technical parts of the course. Sample answers are given in the answer key at the end of each

chapter, but these answers are meant to be suggestive rather than inclusive. The questions and the answers may be useful in written assignments or in classroom discussion.

IV. Chapter Test

The true/false questions in this section will test mastery of the text material. If you feel it is necessary to qualify a statement, be sure to use "false" as the correct answer. The correct answers to these questions are also listed at the end of each chapter. The multiple-choice questions require that you choose the one *best* answer. It would be helpful to make sure that you know *why* the rejected answers are not acceptable.

V. Answers

Answers are given at the end of each chapter for sections two, three, and four.

The answers to the questions are fairly straightforward. The final judges of which answers are correct are the textbook and your instructor. If any question contains an ambiguity (which is always possible in a study guide), a note to the author would be appreciated. I will respond to your question, and future students will be grateful for any clarification that can be made in subsequent editions.

Eleanor D. Craig
Associate Professor of Economics
Department of Economics
University of Delaware

CONTENTS

CHAPTER 1
Scarcity and Choice

CAPSULE SUMMARY

The first chapter introduces many economic concepts, describing them in relation to the basic economic problem in society—unlimited wants in a country with scarce resources. That problem is analyzed through the use of production possibilities curves that define (1) the limits of output available to a country, (2) the costs of choosing one combination of outputs rather than another, and (3) the effects of a change in resource availability or level of use of those resources.

Marginal analysis is introduced, and the different mechanisms for choosing output combinations, either through a market or by command, are reviewed. This chapter summarizes much of the material that forms the basis for the remainder of the text, and it should be studied carefully.

REVIEWING THE CHAPTER

1. A good that is available at no cost and in quantities sufficient for anyone's desires is

   called a/an _____ (free, economic) good. (4)

2. Laissez-faire economics argues that the best economic system is the one that operates

   with the _____ (most, least) government interference. (5)

3. List the four categories of resources: _____

   _____. (6)

4. Unemployment of labor resources causes a _____ (temporary,

   permanent) loss of production to that country. (6)

5. Money is not considered capital because _____

   _____. (6)

6. The three questions every economic system must answer are _____

   goods should be produced, _____ should the resources be combined

   to produce those goods, and _____ should benefit from the

   economy's production. (6–7)

7. _____ economies that organize production have experienced little technological advance and are found in remote sections of less developed countries. (7)

8. A market economy relies on the decisions of _____ (government, individuals) to answer the three basic questions. (8)

9. Give an example of the opportunity cost to you of answering the questions on this page. _____ _____. (8–9)

10. If there are unemployed resources, the economy must be _____ (above, on, underneath) the production possibility curve. (10)

11. Inflation can be defined as a general increase in _____. (11)

12. In a command economy consumer production can be reduced by _____ (executive order, taxation), but in the U.S. economy the best means for reducing consumer production is by _____ (executive order, taxation). (10–11)

13. A production possibility curve that was a straight line (not bowed outward in the middle) would imply that all resources were _____ (equally, not equally) suited for the production of both products. (11)

14. The zero point on a graph is called its _____. (15)

15. Construct a graph showing the probable relationship between miles per gallon of gasoline and size of cars. The relation between these two variables is _____ (direct, inverse), showing that larger cars get _____ (more, fewer) miles per gallon than smaller ones. (15)

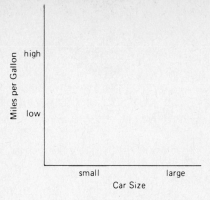

16. Production possibilities curves can shift outward when _____

_____

_____. (16)

17. If the supply of resources available to a particular country decreased, the production

possibilities curve would _____ (shift outward, remain unchanged,

shift inward). (16)

18. List the six essential steps for problem solving in economics. (18–20)

a. _____   d. _____

b. _____   e. _____

c. _____   f. _____

19. The object of the family budgeting analysis is to _____ (maximize,

minimize) the numbers of benefit points available, given an income constraint. (20)

20. If the benefit–cost ratio is _____ (greater than, equal to, less than)

one, the project should be undertaken. (20–21)

SELF-EVALUATION EXERCISES AND APPLICATION

1. Draw a typical production possibilities curve that defines output possibilities for hamburgers and hot dogs. Label two points, A and B, on the production possibility curve and graphically define the opportunity cost of moving from point A to point B. Label another point, C, which represents an underutilization of available resources, and a fourth point, D, which is impossible to attain unless the quantity or quality of resources were increased. Sketch another production possibility curve that would

3

exist if new resources were discovered that were only useful in the production of hot dogs.

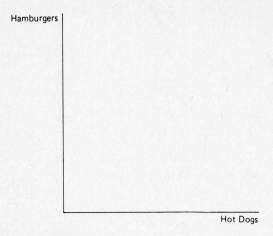

2. Draw another production possibility curve including points on the table below:

Capital Goods	Consumption Goods
110	0
100	20
80	60
30	70
0	75

Consider two countries with identical resources. Country M is producing 100 units of capital goods and 20 units of consumption goods, while Country N is producing 75 units of consumption goods and no capital goods. Since the present production of capital goods will influence the available quantity of resources for the future, sketch two more production possibility curves for that future period—one for Country M and one for Country N on the graph on page 5. What has happened to their relative capacities to produce both capital and consumer goods?

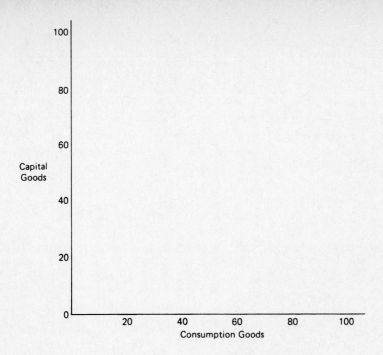

CHAPTER TEST

True/False Questions

T   F   1. Fresh air can be considered an economic good when its price is greater than zero.

T   F   2. If resources were unlimited and desires were limited, the study of economics would not be as important.

T   F   3. The opportunity cost of producing good X decreases as more of that good is manufactured.

T   F   4. Marginal analysis teaches us that the last dollar spent on a given consumer good should generate more benefits than the same dollar spent on any other good.

T   F   5. When one value on a graph increases and the other decreases, the relationship between the two variables is described as inverse.

T   F   6. Benefit–cost calculations cannot account for the benefits or costs that will occur in the future.

T   F   7. At full employment, increasing the production of capital goods requires a decrease in the production of goods for current consumption.

T   F   8. The prices paid to the various factors of production reflect the relative value that society places on the goods that those factors produce.

T   F   9. In a market economy, the consumers "vote" in favor of certain products by spending money on those products.

T   F   10. Social benefits and costs are easier to measure and quantify than private benefits and costs.

Multiple-Choice Questions

1. In economics which of the following are included in the category of resources named "land"?
   a. soil
   b. timber
   c. minerals
   d. water
   e. all of the above

2. A hammer should be considered:
   a. a capital good because it helps labor produce furniture for sale.
   b. a consumption good because it is bought in hardward stores by people who will not use it to produce goods for sale.
   c. both a and b.
   d. a "roundabout" good.
   e. a free good since there are usually more hammers available than are currently being purchased.

3. One of the following is necessary for an economy to be characterized as a command economy:
   a. the economy is trying to improve its military capability.
   b. production is computerized.
   c. the economy is a rapidly growing one.
   d. a central planning agency decides what should be produced and how it should be produced.
   e. taxation is enforced by the government.

4. A given point on a production possibility curve illustrates:
   a. level of production possible only if there is inflation.
   b. an underutilization of economic resources.
   c. the amount of one product that must be given up to increase the output of the other product.
   d. the opportunity cost of producing any quantity of both products.
   e. a direct relationship between the two goods produced.

5. A production possibility curve is usually bowed out in the middle because:
   a. not all resources are equally suitable to produce all goods.
   b. the largest combinations of both goods are near the center where the available resources are used to produce both goods.
   c. the opportunity costs of producing one product increase as the quantity of that product produced increases.
   d. some labor is specialized and produces one product better than other products.
   e. all of the above apply.

6. Which of the following decisions is *not* an example of an economic decision based on marginal analysis?
   a. to study an extra hour rather than to sleep for that hour.
   b. to hire another worker or buy another machine.
   c. to produce another motorcycle or not to produce that motorcycle.
   d. to buy a ticket to a play rather than to buy a steak dinner.
   e. all of the above involve choices at the margin.

7. Social benefits are more difficult to measure than private benefits because:
   a. they are provided by the government.

b. many social projects are not divisible into small units.

c. the benefits typically accrue over a shorter period of time than do private benefits.

d. the costs of a project to the government are usually inflated.

e. none of the above applies.

8. The graph to the right correctly depicts:

a. an inverse relationship between y and x.

b. a direct relationship between y and x.

c. a positive quantity of x when the value of y is zero.

d. a negative quantity of y when x is zero.

e. none of the above is correctly shown.

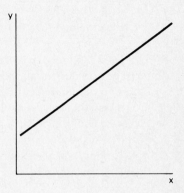

9. Maximizing total benefits from a given income involves:

a. discovering ways to increase the size of the income.

b. deciding which expenditure produces the most satisfaction.

c. comparing one family's expenditure pattern with that of another family.

d. comparing the benefits per dollar spent of each alternative at the margin.

e. comparing the costs of each alternative at the margin.

10. A free-market system, such as that described by Adam Smith in *Wealth of Nations*, does not imply that:

a. producers have to allocate a certain percentage of their profits for capital expenditures.

b. prices determine how resources are used.

c. citizens can choose whether to spend or save their money.

d. consumers can decide which goods give them maximum satisfaction.

e. high salaries in one occupation will attract more workers to that occupation.

11. Both land and capital are nonhuman resources. The difference is that land is:

a. used for government purposes, while capital is not.

b. not manufactured, while capital must be produced.

c. not consumed by production, while capital is used up.

d. usually rented, while capital is privately owned.

e. none of the above.

12. A traditional economy:

a. is apparent in primitive societies.

b. uses little specialization of function.

c. generates relatively small quantities of capital.

d. tends to follow historic patterns.

e. all of the above.

13. An efficient economy is one that:
    a. has low costs of production.
    b. generates large quantities of output.
    c. produces the maximum quantity of output with the minimum quantity of resources.
    d. distributes its output fairly.
    e. uses all resources to generate output.

14. Opportunity cost:
    a. can be illustrated by a production possibility curve.
    b. must be equal for all goods and services chosen.
    c. will be maximized if an economy is producing efficiently.
    d. measures how many inputs are used to produce each good.
    e. measures the benefits to society derived from a given set of production options.

15. A shift in the production possibility curve from _____ to __ __ __ __ __ on the figure below could be caused by:
    a. an increase in labor due to migration.
    b. an improvement in the sanding machine used to produce chairs.
    c. an increase in the number of cattle ready for slaughter.
    d. a shift of resources toward the production of chairs rather than hamburgers.
    e. the invention of a better tasting roll for hamburgers.

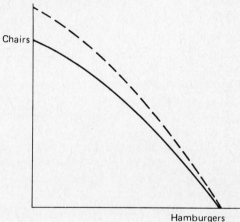

16. Any point on a production possibility curve is technically efficient. The decision as to which point is chosen is called:
    a. *allocation efficiency.*
    b. *opportunity cost.*
    c. *the question of scarcity.*
    d. *efficiency in the distribution of income.*
    e. *choosing at the margin.*

17. *Entrepreneurial ability* is the natural resource that:
    a. is human.
    b. is also called the *creative resource.*
    c. develops the capabilities of other resources.
    d. manages the combination of other resources.
    e. all of the above.

18. It is impossible to move beyond a given production possibilities curve:
    a. unless the allocative choices of society are changed.
    b. without increasing prices of most output.
    c. without increasing opportunity costs.

d. without an increase in available resources.

e. none of the above.

19. Inflation can be described as:

    a. a general increase in prices.

    b. rising relative prices.

    c. increases in prices in one sector of the economy that are offset by decreases in prices in another sector.

    d. rapidly rising prices.

    e. escalation costs.

20. In the year 2000, when we know a great deal more about the nation's economy, we will probably witness:

    a. the end of scarcity.

    b. a time when people do not have to make choices.

    c. an economy without markets.

    d. unlimited resources.

    e. none of the above.

ANSWERS

Reviewing the Chapter

1. free
2. least
3. labor, entrepreneurial ability, land, capital
4. permanent
5. money by itself cannot produce other goods
6. what, how, who
7. traditional
8. individuals
9. examples are another course not studied, a conversation with a friend missed, another hour of sleep sacrificed
10. underneath
11. prices
12. both executive order and taxation, taxation
13. equally
14. origin
15. inverse, fewer
16. technology advances, resources increase in supply
17. shift inward
18. a. define the problem; b. specify the goals; c. identify the economic concepts involved; d. list the alternative choices available; e. evaluate each alternative; f. decide which alternative is best
19. maximize
20. greater than

Self-Evaluation Exercises and Applications

1. The opportunity cost of moving from point A to point B is $Q_2 - Q_1$ worth of hamburgers.

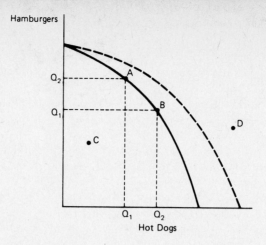

2. Country M's production possibility curve will shift out and to the right, as shown by the broken line in the figure below. Country N's curve will still be defined by the solid line, indicating no increase in capacity to produce capital or consumer goods.

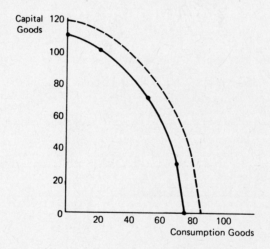

Chapter Test

True/False Questions

1. true	4. true	7. true	10. false
2. true	5. true	8. true	
3. false	6. false	9. true	

Multiple-Choice Questions

1. e; 2. c; 3. d; 4. c; 5. e; 6. e; 7. b; 8. b; 9. d; 10. a; 11. b; 12. e; 13. c; 14. a; 15. b; 16. a; 17. e; 18. d; 19. a; 20. e.

CHAPTER 2

Demand

CAPSULE SUMMARY

Demand describes the relation between prices of goods and quantities that buyers will purchase. Important concepts include how responsive the buyers are to price changes, whether markets can be separated so that different prices can be charged for the same good, and how demand responds when other circumstances change.

Those circumstances that affect demand include levels of income, numbers of buyers, the availability and price of substitute and complementary goods, and the tastes of the buyers. When one of these circumstances changes, the entire demand curve will shift, indicating a different quantity demanded at *every* price.

REVIEWING THE CHAPTER

1. Adam Smith argued that a free market acted like a/an _____ in that if each individual were allowed to pursue his own self-interest, the maximum economic benefits would result for the entire society. (25)

2. If a firm is small relative to the market and cannot affect the price for which it sells its product, it is called a _____ taker. (26)

3. Microeconomics studies the relation between consumer _____ (demand, supply) and producer _____ (demand, supply). (26)

4. A decrease in price results in an increase in _____ (demand, quantity demanded), whereas an increase in the number of consumers results in an increase in _____ (demand, quantity demanded). (30)

5. A substitute good is one that _____

    _____

    _____. (31)

    List possible substitutes for these goods:

    a. sneakers

b. radial tires

c. pretzels

A complementary good is one that is used _____ with another good. List complements to the above goods a through c. (31)

6. The law of demand states that as price _____ (decreases, increases) the _____ demanded will increase. (27)

7. If demand is _____ (elastic, inelastic), an increase in price will result in a decrease in total _____. (28)

8. The demand schedule for a single product represents the horizontal addition of the _____ for that product in a market. (26–27)

9. If total revenue increases as price is increased, there must be movement _____ (up, down) the demand curve. (27–28)

10. If demand is completely inelastic, raising the price will always result in an _____ of total revenue. (28–29)

11. Demand is more elastic over longer periods of time because _____ _____ _____. (29)

12. If consumer income falls, the demand curve for most goods will shift _____. (30)

13. If each shoe in a pair were priced separately, an increase in the price of left shoes would shift the demand curve for right shoes to the _____ (right, left). (31)

14. Elasticity of demand can be measured by comparing the _____ change in quantity generated by a given percentage change in price. (33)

15. Firms do not operate to maximize total revenue. They must also consider the _____ of producing the output. (36)

16. Price _____ is the practice of selling the same product for more than a single price. (37)

17. Sometimes restaurants will have "ladies nights" and charge lower prices for food and beverages to females. This form of differential pricing might be advantageous if _____. (37–39)

18. Airline passengers with business meetings in different cities are likely to have relatively _____ (elastic, inelastic) demands for air travel. (38–39)

19. Taxes imposed on a consumer good that is considered a necessity will produce _____ (less, more) revenue for the government than those imposed on a good where the quantity demanded is _____ (less, more) responsive to price changes. (39)

20. The demand for a single farm product is _____ (less, more) elastic than the demand for all farm products. (36)

SELF-EVALUATION EXERCISES AND APPLICATIONS

1. Market studies have shown that an increase in the price of gasoline by 25 cents per gallon will decrease consumption of gasoline by only 5% in the first and second years. However, by the fifth year, the quantity consumed is expected to decrease by 30%. What kinds of adjustments could producers and consumers of transportation make in the long run to this price increase that would not be possible in the short run? For example—changes in car sizes, alternative forms of transportation, and alternative energy sources for automobiles.

CHAPTER TEST

True/False Questions

T   F   1. Rebates to encourage car purchases would result in an increase in the demand for cars.

T	F	2.	A vertical demand curve may be described as perfectly inelastic.
T	F	3.	Artificially low prices on gasoline have encouraged the use of large cars since cars and gasoline are complementary goods.
T	F	4.	Total revenue will always increase when prices fall.
T	F	5.	A large migration of people to this country will tend to shift the demand curve for most products out and to the right.
T	F	6.	If the elasticity of demand is −2.0, we know that a decrease in price will generate lower revenue.
T	F	7.	Tickets to the same ice hockey game are sold for different prices. The more expensive tickets enable spectators to sit closer to the ice. Without ushers and assigned seats, it would be difficult to get anyone to purchase the more expensive tickets.
T	F	8.	Some new cars sell for $25,000, whereas the average sticker price on automobiles is less than $10,000. This is a good example of price discrimination.
T	F	9.	A tax on a good with a relatively elastic demand curve will be a good revenue producer for the government.
T	F	10.	A good example of two complementary goods is light bulbs and jeans.

Multiple-Choice Questions

1. Perfect competition in a market assumes that:
   a. all buyers and sellers can determine their own prices.
   b. all buyers and sellers must accept the prices set by the market.
   c. buyers and sellers are few in number.
   d. each producer manufactures a unique product.
   e. none of the above are essential assumptions for competition.

2. A demand curve gives a relationship between price and quantity demanded, other things equal. These "other things" include all of the following except:
   a. tastes.
   b. distribution of income.
   c. quantity supplied at every price.
   d. the price of substitute products.
   e. the price of complementary products.

3. Recently the demand curve for bicycles has shifted rapidly to the right. Which of the following would *not* provide a possible explanation for this shift:
   a. increases in the price of cars.
   b. increases in the number of children in the bicycle-riding ages.
   c. the discovery that exercise prevents heart attacks.
   d. a decrease in the price of bicycles.
   e. all of the above are reasonable explanations.

4. Suppose the subway fare in a city is raised from 15 cents per ride to 25 cents per ride while the bus fare is unchanged at 15 cents. How would total fare revenue be affected by the subway fare increase:
   a. it would increase for buses but might increase or decrease for subways.
   b. it would increase for subways but might increase or decrease for buses.
   c. it would increase for both subways and buses.

    d.   it would decrease for both subways and buses.

    e.   it would remain unchanged for both subways and buses.

5.   Rank the demand curves in the diagram below in order of greatest to least elasticity at the common intersection point:

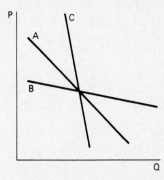

    a.   A, B, C.

    b.   B, C, A.

    c.   B, A, C.

    d.   C, A, B.

    e.   none are correct orderings.

6.   If consumers have budgeted a fixed amount of money to buy a certain commodity, and within a certain range of prices will spend neither more nor less than this amount on it, then their demand curve in this price range could be called:

    a.   in equilibrium.

    b.   perfectly elastic.

    c.   perfectly inelastic.

    d.   highly inelastic but not perfectly so.

    e.   responsive to price changes.

7.   Demand curve A is more elastic than demand curve B if:

    a.   there are few substitutes for A, many for B.

    b.   good A is a necessity, B a luxury.

    c.   purchasing good A takes a large percentage of total income; good B, a small percentage.

    d.   good B is more durable than good A.

    e.   goods A and B are complements for each other.

8.   Suppose that commodities A and B are *complements* for one another in consumption, and the price of B rises sharply due to curtailed supply. Which of the following will occur:

    a.   the amount demanded of A will tend to rise.

    b.   the price of A will tend to fall.

    c.   both the price of A and the quantity demanded of A will tend to rise.

    d.   the price of A will tend to rise, and the quantity demanded will tend to fall.

    e.   the price of A will tend to fall, and the quantity demanded will tend to rise.

9.   A tax on cigarettes and a tax on alcoholic beverages are similar in that:

    a.   they are relatively good at producing revenue for the government.

    b.   the demand for both goods is relatively inelastic.

    c.   the tax will not discourage consumption by very much.

    d.   the quantity demanded varies little as the price increases.

    e.   all of the above.

10. Adam Smith argued that the "invisible hand":
    a. should be directed by government.
    b. always resulted in an equitable (or fair) distribution of income.
    c. directed markets to provide the maximum economic benefits to all people.
    d. could be relied upon to direct consumer choices.
    e. determined the location of the production possibilities curve.
11. Which of the following conditions is *not* necessary if markets work in an ideal manner:
    a. there must be many buyers and sellers.
    b. the buyers and sellers must be price takers.
    c. the products in each market must be nearly identical.
    d. buyers and producers must know the conditions existing in each market.
    e. consumers are required to buy from a single producer.
12. Demand and supply curves:
    a. are a model of a market.
    b. usually slope upward and toward the right.
    c. are pictures of total revenues and total costs of producing a product.
    d. rarely intersect.
    e. indicate that quantity is inversely related to price.
13. Total revenue can be measured by the:
    a. entire area under a supply curve.
    b. quantity of production.
    c. profits of a firm.
    d. entire area under a demand curve.
    e. price times the quantity produced.
14. Which of the following characteristics is likely to make a demand curve more elastic:
    a. if the good is a necessity.
    b. insensitivity of quantity demanded to price.
    c. if the good has numerous substitutes.
    d. if it's difficult to postpone the purchase of that good.
    e. if the good accounts for a very small part of the buyer's budget.
15. Anticipating a price decrease will tend to:
    a. increase current demand.
    b. reduce current demand.
    c. cause a movement down a given demand curve.
    d. cause a movement up a given demand curve.
    e. none of the above.
16. The main reason why Americans want smaller cars is that:
    a. they are trying to copy the European and Japanese models.
    b. the prices of substitutes have been lowered.
    c. there were gasoline lines several years ago.
    d. small cars are safer.
    e. the relative price of a complementary good (gasoline) has risen rapidly.
17. If the following prices and quantities are from a demand curve, what is the elasticity of demand between those two points?

	price	quantity
a. −1.13	$10	4
b. −0.88	7	6
c. −1.70		
d. −2.50		
e. none of the above		

18. The elasticity of demand is likely to be greater when:
    a. quantities are small.
    b. prices are high.
    c. the p and quantity are near the left-hand portion of the demand curve.
    d. total revenue increases if price is dropped.
    e. all of the above.

19. Total revenue is maximized where:
    a. the elasticity of demand is one.
    b. profits are maximized.
    c. the demand curve is downward sloping to the right.
    d. the demand curve is parallel to the x-axis.
    e. the supply curve crosses the demand curve.

20. An example of price discrimination is:
    a. higher prices for seats closer to the performers at a concert.
    b. higher prices during weekdays for telephone calls.
    c. higher prices for first-class seats in airplanes.
    d. lower price theater tickets purchased at the last minute.
    e. all of the above.

ANSWERS

Reviewing the Chapter

1. invisible hand
2. price
3. demand, supply
4. quantity demanded, demand
5. can be used in place of another, increases in demand when the price of its substitute increases; together
6. decreases, quantity
7. elastic, revenue
8. demand curves for each individual person
9. up
10. increase
11. there is adequate time to find substitutes
12. to the left
13. left
14. percentage
15. costs
16. discrimination
17. it increased the number of female customers without reducing the male purchasers
18. inelastic
19. more, more
20. more

Self-Evaluation Exercises and Applications

1. Possible adjustments to increased gasoline prices available in the long run might include:
   a. purchases of smaller cars.
   b. building of more mass transit.
   c. electrical generating power for cars.
   d. formation of car pools.
   e. increased gas efficiency in cars.
   f. people moving closer to their employment and schools.
   g. fewer undergraduate commuters.

Chapter Test

True/False Questions

1. false	4. false	7. true	10. false
2. true	5. true	8. false	
3. true	6. false	9. false	

Multiple-Choice Questions

1. b; 2. c; 3. d; 4. a; 5. c; 6. c; 7. c; 8. b; 9. e; 10. c; 11. e; 12. a; 13. e; 14. c; 15. b; 16. e; 17. a; 18. e; 19. a; 20. e.

CHAPTER 3

Supply and Market Equilibrium

CAPSULE SUMMARY

Supply speaks exclusively to the combination of quantities and prices that will be chosen by producers. A normal supply curve contains a direct relationship between price and quantity, indicating that an increase in price induces an increase in the quantity supplied.

The location of a single supply curve is a function of the number of producers, the level of technology, the costs of resources, and the expectations of price changes for the product.

The steepness (elasticity) of a supply curve depends primarily on the good's ability to be stored and the time period that it takes to change the productive capacity of firms.

Equilibrium in a market is found where the demand and supply curves cross, creating a single price and quantity that pleases both buyers and sellers. In economics this point is called efficient because it represents an optimum allocation of resources. Any non-equilibrium price is inefficient, and the chapter deals with several examples of non-equilibrium prices.

REVIEWING THE CHAPTER

1. The payments to those who provide resources for production include

    _____ for workers, _____

    for land, _____ for capital, and _____ for en-

    trepreneurs. (44)

2. _____ profits are necessary to keep entrepreneurs in their existing

    lines of business, whereas _____ profits are profits that exceed the

    necessary profits. (44)

3. _____ (Variable, Fixed) costs increase as the quantity of output is in-

    creased. (44–45)

4. Average fixed costs _____ (increase, decrease, remain constant) as

    output increases. (45)

5. Goods that are easily stored are more likely to have a _____ (more,

    less) elastic supply curve. (50)

6. _____ are total costs divided by quantity produced. (46)

7. Production will always be _____ (increased, decreased) if marginal revenue exceeds marginal costs, as long as marginal revenue also exceeds the _____. (47)

8. Supply is more _____ (elastic, inelastic) in the short run than it is over a longer period of time. (50)

9. The difference between an individual firm's supply curve and that for a market is _____. (48–49)

10. The normal relation between the quantity supplied and the price is _____ (inverse, direct), that is, as the price increases, the quantity supplied _____ (increases, decreases). (48)

11. Draw a supply curve that indicates fixed supply, or perfectly inelastic supply, on graph (a). Draw a supply curve on graph (b) that is perfectly elastic. Draw a supply curve on graph (c) that illustrates more usual elasticity. (50)

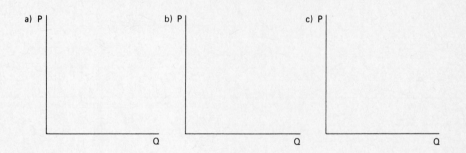

12. Describe the shifts in the supply or demand curves for orange juice that are likely to be caused by: (26–31, (43–51)

Event	Curve Affected	Direction of Effect	Probable Direction of Price Change
a. American income increase:	_____	_____	_____
b. price of fertilizer increases:	_____	_____	_____
c. price of oranges increases:	_____	_____	_____
d. price of grapefruit falls:	_____	_____	_____
e. an advertising campaign by the Citrus Association succeeds in convincing people of the importance of Vitamin C:	_____	_____	_____

13. A shortage occurs in a market when the quantity _____ (demanded, supplied) exceeds the quantity _____ (demanded, supplied) at a price _____ (above, below) equilibrium. (52)

14. On the graph below show with a bracket the quantity of excess supply (surplus in the market) if the price were set at P_1. What would the surplus be if the price were set at P_2. (51–52)

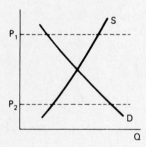

Show the excess demand (shortage) at P_2 and at P_1.

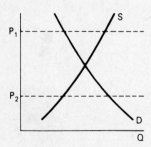

15. The National Energy Act passed in October 1978 will gradually remove the price ceilings on natural gas. This should result in a/an _____ (decrease, increase) in the quantity demanded, a/an _____ (decrease, increase) in the quantity supplied, and a _____ (lower, higher) price. (57)

16. An increase in the number of firms in an industry will cause a _____ _____ (movement along, shift in) the supply curve. (49–50)

17. Supply is likely to be _____ (more, less) elastic if it takes a long while for firms to add productive capacity. (50–51)

18. Economic profits are _____ (greater than, less than) normal profits. (44)

SELF-EVALUATION EXERCISES AND APPLICATIONS

1. If the price of domestic oil is held at $8.53 per barrel by legislation and the market price is $13.31 per barrel, what would you expect to happen to the quantity demanded and the quantity supplied? What problems would this pose for an economy? How could these problems be corrected?

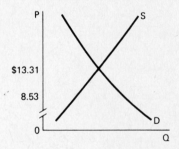

2. Supply and demand:
   a. Draw a demand and a supply curve from the following data:

Demand for Candy Canes per Month		Supply of Candy Canes per Month	
Price	Quantity	Price	Quantity
5	6	1	13
4	12	2	31
3	23	3	43
2	31	4	47
1	45	5	50

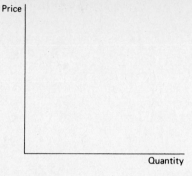

Price

Quantity

b. At what price is there excess demand? How much?

c. Where is market equilibrium? Why?

d. What is the likely effect on price if:
   (1) supply increases and demand decreases?
   (2) demand increases and supply decreases?
   (3) demand increases and supply increases?
   (4) supply decreases and demand remains constant?

e. What would happen to the curves if:
   (1) the candy cane eating population grew?
   (2) the cost of producing candy canes fell?
   (3) demand for candy canes increases when the price falls?
   (4) candy cane prices go up so that most families switch to licorice sticks?

3. If a firm mistakenly decided to charge for their product a price that was higher than equilibrium price, what indications would the firm have that this price was too high? What would probably happen? What if the price were lower than equilibrium?

4. Severe weather (e.g., heavy and prolonged snowstorms) often generates atypical demand and supply situations. What shifts in the entire demand and supply curves might be predicted from such weather conditions?

5. The simplifying assumptions defining our typical firm in a market are: (1) firms have no control over the price they charge; (2) the products these firms produce are identical, or nearly so; and (3) all firms have perfect knowledge of selling conditions throughout the market. Can you think of situations where these assumptions do not hold up in the "real" world? Suggest a few.

CHAPTER TEST

True/False Questions

T   F   1. A supply curve shows all the quantities that will be bought at various market prices.

T   F   2. In a free market the equilibrium price for a good is that price where all goods in all markets have the same price.

T   F   3. If the price is artificially maintained at a level that is lower than equilibrium, the value to the consumer of the quantity that will be produced will exceed the marginal costs to the supplier.

T   F   4. One of the explanations for the direct relation between price and quantity supplied is that consumers will pay a higher price for more goods.

T   F   5. An increase in resource prices will cause the supply curve to shift to the right.

T   F   6. If the supply of a product falls, given the demand, price will decrease and quantity will decrease.

T   F   7. At full employment, the only way to increase the production of public goods is to decrease the production of private goods.

T   F   8. Price floors for agricultural products have encouraged shortages in grain markets.

T   F   9. Supply curves tend to be much more elastic in the long run.

T   F   10. The supply of housing tends to be very inelastic in the short run.

Multiple-Choice Questions

1. Economic profits are those that:
    a. equal normal profits.
    b. exceed normal profits.
    c. are necessary profits.
    d. include all profits.
    e. are total payments to entrepreneurs.

2. Fixed costs include:
    a. those that don't change as the quantity of output increases.
    b. charges for plant and heavy machinery.
    c. managerial personnel's income.

d. mortgage payments.

e. all of the above.

3. The change in total costs caused by the production of a single extra unit of output is called:

a. average cost.   d. average total cost.

b. average variable cost.   e. none of the above.

c. marginal cost.

4. A firm will produce:

a. less if marginal revenue exceeds marginal costs.

b. more if marginal revenue exceeds marginal costs.

c. more if marginal costs exceed marginal revenue.

d. less if total revenue is less than total costs.

e. none of the above.

5. A firm in competition:

a. can sell as much as it wishes at existing market prices.

b. has marginal revenue that equals price.

c. will choose to sell where marginal revenue equals marginal costs, as long as average variable costs are covered.

d. is a price taker.

e. all of the above.

6. The marginal cost curve becomes a firm's supply curve:

a. as long as it's positively sloped.

b. above the average variable cost curve.

c. where MC = MR.

d. at all points.

e. at quantities where the firm will earn economic profits.

7. A reduction in costs of an input would be graphed as a/an:

a. decrease in supply.

b. increase in supply.

c. decrease in demand.

d. increase in demand.

e. movement along a given supply curve.

8. What effect would an increase in oil prices by the OPEC countries have on U.S. *coal* producers:

a. the supply of coal would decrease, causing prices and profits to rise.

b. demand for coal would increase, causing prices and profits to rise.

c. the supply of coal would decrease, causing prices and profits to fall.

d. the demand for coal would decrease, causing prices and profits to fall.

e. the supply of coal would increase, causing prices and profits to rise.

9. Increasing the time period under consideration will usually:

a. shift the supply curve.

b. make the supply curve more elastic.

c. cause a movement along a supply curve.

d. reduce equilibrium price.

e. generate a surplus.

10. Which of the following statements is *incorrect* (Hint: try to draw diagrams.):
    a. if supply declines and demand remains constant, equilibrium price will rise.
    b. if demand decreases and supply increases, equilibrium price will rise.
    c. if supply increases and demand decreases, equilibrium price will fall.
    d. if demand increases and supply decreases, price will rise.
    e. if supply increases and demand remains constant, equilibrium price will fall.
11. The whole supply curve will shift to the left if:
    a. production costs decrease.
    b. the number of firms in the industry increases.
    c. there is a new invention that makes the production process more efficient.
    d. people expect that the price of the product would fall.
    e. none of the above.
12. Equilibrium price is:
    a. the only price that both demanders and suppliers want.
    b. inflationary because it is uncontrolled.
    c. rarely achieved in the real world.
    d. a price that usually generates surpluses.
    e. the price that produces normal, but not economic, profits.
13. Price ceilings are often used when:
    a. prices are thought to be too low so that an insufficient supply is produced.
    b. prices are thought to be too low so that consumers want more than is supplied.
    c. frictions and immobilities prolong the transition to changed supply and demand conditions.
    d. prices are thought to be too high so that consumers want too little of a worthwhile product.
    e. prices are thought to be too high so that producers supply more than is wanted.
14. Target prices for farm products are:
    a. set at equilibrium.
    b. set to cover basic costs of production.
    c. unnecessary with low demand for farm products.
    d. often used to help bolster supply.
    e. the cause of unstable farm incomes.
15. Efficiency occurs when:
    a. equilibrium prices prevail.
    b. the quantity supplied equals the quantity demanded.
    c. scarce resources are used to produce the most production possible.
    d. the price charged by producers is the same as the price paid by consumers.
    e. all of the above.
16. If market prices are increasing, a possible cause would be:
    a. a reduction in supply accompanied by an increase in demand.
    b. a decrease in demand.
    c. an increase in demand accompanied by an increase in supply.
    d. an increase in supply.
    e. none of the above.
17. A price control is much more likely to restrict production if:
    a. supply is relatively elastic.

b. demand is relatively inelastic.

c. supply is relatively inelastic.

d. demand and supply are relatively inelastic.

e. none of the above.

18. Demand is relatively inelastic for all farm products. However, the demand for most single commodities is relatively elastic. This is because:

   a. the demand for a single commodity is a function of the other goods with which it is used.

   b. single commodities use only a small portion of the budget of a consumer.

   c. there are good substitutes for single commodities.

   d. there can be widespread crop failures for single products.

   e. production plans for most single commodities are made six months to a year before the crop is marketed.

19. Mortgages are a complement to housing demand, as most houses must be purchased with borrowed funds. When interest rates are high over a long period of time, the housing market will experience:

   a. a decrease in demand.

   b. a decrease in the quantity supplied.

   c. a decrease in relative prices of housing.

   d. a decrease in the number of houses purchased.

   e. all of the above.

20. The elasticity of supply is likely to be greater:

   a. when there are good substitutes.

   b. when there are a fixed number of firms.

   c. when purchasers become more wealthy.

   d. in the long run.

   e. in the short run.

ANSWERS

Reviewing the Chapter

1. wages and salaries, rent, interest, profits
2. normal, economic
3. variable
4. decrease
5. more
6. average total costs
7. increased, average variable cost
8. inelastic
9. the market supply is the sum of all the individual firm's supply curves
10. direct, increase

11.

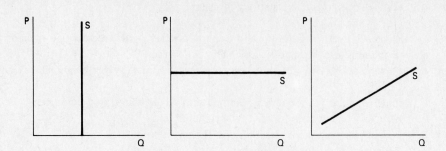

a)   b)   c)

12.

Curve Affected	Direction of Effect	Direction of Price Change
a. demand	to right	increase
b. supply	to right	decrease
c. neither	——	——
d. demand	to left	decrease
e. demand	to right	increase

13. demanded, supplied, below
14. surplus at P_1
    surplus at P_2 – none
    shortage at P_1 – none
    shortage at P_2

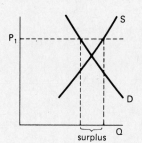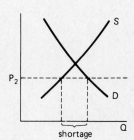

15. decrease, increase, higher
16. shift in
17. less
18. greater than

SELF-EVALUATION EXERCISES AND APPLICATIONS

1. The quantity demanded would be greater
    than equilibrium quantity, and the quantity
    supplied would be less than the equilibrium
    quantity. The problems that this would pose
    for the economy might include:

    a. shortages of oil.
    b. production of cars that are bigger than
        if oil prices were higher.
    c. more use of oil heat than substitute
        energy forms for heating.
    d. more use of oil for generating
        electricity than coal or nuclear power.
    e. fewer new oil wells discovered in the U.S.
    f. more oil imports if imported prices are higher than $8.53.
        The economic solution to all of these problems is to allow the price to reach
        equilibrium.

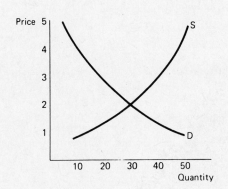

2. a.

    b. There is excess demand at P = 1 of 32 candy canes.
    c. Market equilibrium is at P = 2 and Q = 31 because the quantity demanded
        equals the quantity supplied.
    d. Price will:
        (1) fall.
        (2) rise.
        (3) can rise or fall depending on how large the shifts in the supply and demand
             curves are.
        (4) rise.
    e. Effect will be to:
        (1) shift demand curve out and to the right.
        (2) shift supply curve out and to the right.

(3) make no change in curves themselves, describe a movement along a given demand curve (e.g., from point A to B).

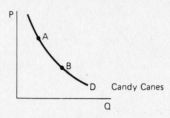

(4) cause movement along a curve (e.g., from point B to A above) but would also result in shifting the demand curve for licorice sticks out and to the right.

3. A price higher than equilibrium would result in unplanned build-up of inventories (i.e., excess supply). To get rid of these extra products, the firm would have to lower the price. If the price was lower than equilibrium, the firm would be facing excess demand for its product and couldn't produce enough output to satisfy the demand at that price.

4. Severe weather might result in factory closings and shortages of raw materials, thus decreasing the supply of many products. The adverse weather conditions might also decrease demand if consumers were unable to get to the stores. The demand for storm-related items might increase (e.g., snow shovels, sleds, and salt).

5. The simplifying assumptions don't hold up when firms have some control over prices (e.g., the only grocery store in a small town, the only utility serving a region). Product differentiation is frequently used as a means of attracting business (e.g., the hamburger chains with a particular type of roll, or extras served with the hamburger). It is certainly questionable whether all firms know the selling conditions throughout the market, including resource prices and substitute product prices.

Chapter Test

True/False Questions

1. false	4. false	7. true	10. true
2. false	5. true	8. false	
3. true	6. false	9. true	

Multiple-Choice Questions

1. b; 2. e; 3. c; 4. b; 5. e; 6. b; 7. b; 8. b; 9. b; 10. b; 11. e; 12. a; 13. c; 14. b; 15. e; 16. a; 17. a; 18. c; 19. e; 20. d.

CHAPTER 4

Market Adjustments With and Without Competition

CAPSULE SUMMARY

In competitive markets, economic profit acts as a signal to encourage new firms to enter a market. As new firms start to produce, the supply curve for the industry shifts to the right, increasing quantity and reducing the price. This adjustment will continue until economic profits are zero.

However, in some markets competition does not exist, in the sense that firms do not have to accept the market price. Rather, noncompetitive firms can decide which price will maximize their profits. Since entry is restricted, that price may be high enough to allow positive economic profits.

This chapter examines several types of noncompetitive industries and reviews methods that are used by government in an attempt to guarantee market results that are in the best interests of society.

REVIEWING THE CHAPTER

1. Profits take two forms: _____ profits, which are the minimum payment necessary to keep managerial ability working in a given type of business, and _____ profits, which act as a signal to resources and indicate the high demand for the products of that business. (65–66)

2. In a competitive industry, if price exceeds production costs, new firms will enter the industry and the supply curve will shift to the _____ (left, right). (66)

3. _____ profits will tend to encourage firms to leave that particular industry. (66)

4. Perfect monopoly describes the case where there is _____ firm that produces all the output for a given industry. (67)

5. Price _____ are a type of monopoly in which several firms are responsible for the market price of a particular good and have the power to continue to sell their product when they raise their price. (68)

6. There are _____ (many, few) industries that can be characterized as perfect monopolies. Yet there are _____ (many, few) industries where several firms have considerable power to "make prices." (67)

7. _____ integration includes firms that produce the same product at the same stage of production (e.g., two wholesalers). _____ integration includes firms that combine several stages of production (e.g., wholesaling and manufacturing). (68)

8. List two ways that firms in monopolistic competition will try to differentiate their product from other similar products. (69)

   a. _____

   b. _____

9. List several reasons why economic profits do not automatically induce new firms to start producing a product where there is some monopoly power. (69)

   a. _____

   b. _____

   c. _____

10. The Clayton Act of 1914 prohibited specific anticompetitive actions, such as _____, whereby a firm charges different prices for the same product; _____, under which a firm insists that purchasers of one product must also buy its complementary product from the same firm; and _____, where a single person would serve on the board of directors of several "competing" companies. (72–73)

11. A business merger that combines firms from totally unrelated industries is called a/an _____. (73)

12. The competitive price at equilibrium is always where the quantity demanded equals the quantity _____. (77)

13. A monopolist may charge a price above the competitive price to increase his

_____ (economic, normal) profit or to increase his total

_____ (sales, revenue). (77)

14. When there is oligopoly, the market leader will encourage price stability by refusing

to follow price _____ (increases, decreases) by the other firms and

thus increasing sales and by undercutting price _____ (increases,

decreases) and also increasing sales. (78)

15. In oligopoly when there is an increase in demand, the _____ (quanti-

ty, quantity and price, price) will increase. This compares with competition, where an

increase in demand will result in an increase in _____ (quantity,

quantity and price, price). (79)

16. A good example of a natural monopoly is _____. (79)

17. A regulated monopoly may be encouraged to use price _____

in its rate schedule, if the result is to help the firm cover full costs of production. (79)

18. Total revenues are greater when a firm can charge several different prices than if a

firm can only charge one price because _____

_____. (79–80)

19. If an electrical utility is forced to charge lower rates for its electricity than those suffi-

cient to cover the full costs of production, that utility may not be able to provide suf-

ficient incentive for _____ to furnish the firm with funds for capital

expansion. (80)

SELF-EVALUATION EXERCISES AND APPLICATIONS

1. With demand and supply curves, illustrate the following events in a competitive industry:
   a. tastes change so that demand increases.
   b. equilibrium price and quantity change—show on
      diagram as a result of (a).
   c. new firms enter the market and begin producing this
      good—show on diagram.
   d. equilibrium price and quantity change—again, show on
      diagram as a result of (c).
   e. After this adjustment process is completed, how high
      are economic profits?

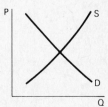

2. Answer the same questions from exercise 1, except this time assume that there is only one firm in the industry with full monopoly power.

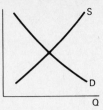

3. Electricity rates have been the subject of much discussion for the past few years. Many people believe that lower rates should be offered to poor people, at least for a minimum level of usage. Such rates are called "lifeline" rates. Assess the results of using a "lifeline" rate structure on:

   a. the quantity of electricity demanded by people with low incomes.

   b. the rate that all other users would have to pay.

   c. the prices of products that use electricity in their production process (some of which are bought by low-income people).

   d. the conservation of electricity.

   e. the ability of poor people to function in today's economy.

   f. the rate of return on investment in this utility.

4. Show on the following demand curves the total revenue generated by: (a) a single price and (b) a pricing scheme that charged a different price for every unit sold (i.e., perfect price discrimination).

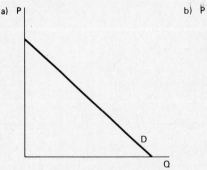
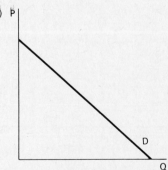

CHAPTER TEST

True/False Questions

T F 1. If economic profits are zero, market prices are exactly equal to the full costs of production.

T F 2. A single oligopolist has less power over price and quantity sold than does a single monopolist.

T F 3. A perfectly competitive firm cannot expand production without lowering the price of its product.

T F 4. Expanding sales always increases the total revenue of a monopolist.

T F 5. If a monopolist charges a higher price for a product than would be charged by a competitor, the opportunity costs of buying that product have increased.

T F 6. Most stockholders in major corporations play an active role in managing the companies in which they hold stock.

T F 7. Good examples of oligopolistic industries are automobiles, farm products, and steel producers.

T F 8. Monopoly in a given industry interferes with the ability of prices to adjust automatically to changes in demand or costs.

T F 9. Most economists would argue that there is never a legitimate justification for allowing a single producer in a given industry.

T F 10. In natural monopolies it is *not* difficult for the regulators to determine a "fair" rate schedule.

Multiple-Choice Questions

1. In a competitive industry where there are negative economic profits:
   a. resources will move to other industries.
   b. firms will go out of business.
   c. the price of the product will be too low to cover the costs of production.
   d. the total supply of output in this industry will decrease.
   e. all of the above will occur.

2. Competitive markets result in the most efficient use of resources because:
   a. consumers will not purchase goods if their prices are too high.
   b. producers will not manufacture goods if economic profits are not sufficiently high.
   c. the competitive price will be the lowest price at which the good can be produced.
   d. monopolists can't be forced to produce at low prices.
   e. in the short run, firms can never earn positive economic profits.

3. Monopolistic competitors have:
   a. truly unique products.
   b. products that are very similar to those of other firms.
   c. power to set prices as high as they wish without losing sales.
   d. no power to raise prices without losing sales.
   e. none of the above are characteristics of monopolistic competitors.

4. Total revenue will always decrease when:
   a. less is produced if the firm is a monopolist.

    b. less is produced if the firm is an oligopolist.
    c. more is produced if the firm is a monopolistic competitor.
    d. more is produced if the firm is a competitor.
    e. less is produced if the firm is a competitor.

5. The Sherman Antitrust Act of 1890:
    a. prevented business mergers.
    b. was only used against big business.
    c. was easy for the courts to interpret.
    d. prohibited price discrimination.
    e. was the first major legislation outlawing trusts.

6. A business merger that combined a MacDonald's and a Gino's outlet would be called:
    a. a conglomerate.
    b. horizontal integration.
    c. vertical integration.
    d. a tying contract.
    e. all of the above could be appropriate descriptions.

7. Not all "bigness" in firm size generates "badness" in economic results because:
    a. the U.S. market for products is very large.
    b. the government carefully watches "big" firms and prevents them from becoming "bad."
    c. most manufactured goods can only be produced by very large firms.
    d. large firms frequently have lower unit costs due to their large production volume.
    e. large firms are usually profitable.

8. A monopolist will probably:
    a. charge a higher price than a competitive firm producing the same product.
    b. produce a smaller quantity than a competitive firm producing the same product.
    c. not worry about entry of new firms if the monopolist firm is earning economic profits.
    d. cause the opportunity costs of buying, and thus the resources used, to be greater for the product than if the product were sold competitively.
    e. all of the above are descriptive of a monopolist.

9. Natural monopolies are *not* characterized by:
    a. governmental regulation.
    b. heavy fixed costs (i.e., costs that don't vary as the quantity of output changes).
    c. one firm in each industry.
    d. public ownership of the resources used in the industry.
    e. all of the above are characteristics of natural monopolies.

10. Positive economic profits:
    a. encourage resources to work for that industry.
    b. encourage new firms to enter that industry.
    c. can't exist in perfect competition for a long time period.
    d. may result from an increase in demand for the products of that industry.
    e. all of the above describe positive economic profits.

11. When economic profits exist, a well-functioning market will cause:
    a. an expansion of production.
    b. a shift outward of the entire supply curve.

c. a downward pressure on price.

d. a reduction of economic profits.

e. all of the above.

12. Efficient production implies:

a. well-functioning markets.

b. benefits that exceed costs.

c. costs that exceed benefits.

d. the use of the most costly way of satisfying consumer wants.

e. that the government tells producers what to supply.

13. Gentlemen's agreements do *not:*

a. replicate monopoly markets.

b. establish market shares for each participant.

c. result in competitive pricing policies.

d. end up with results similar to those of price makers.

e. result in higher prices and/or less quantity than competitive markets.

14. Competitive markets achieve many desirable effects. One advantage would be:

a. equity in the distribution of income.

b. prices that just cover costs of production in the long run.

c. few firms in each market.

d. economic profits for all firms.

e. higher prices and less production than noncompetitive firms would choose.

15. Oligopolies and monopolies are similar in that:

a. there are numerous producers.

b. prices are higher and quantity sold is lower than in competitive business.

c. both types of firms attempt to maximize profits.

d. both types of firms attempt to minimize costs.

e. they both encourage economic efficiency.

16. Changes in market conditions are more likely to be reflected in:

a. prices in competitive industries.

b. prices in monopolistic industries.

c. output quantities in oligopolistic industries.

d. employment in monopolistic industries.

e. none of the above.

17. Price discrimination for electrical utilities:

a. is normally regulated.

b. allows several different prices to be charged for the same product.

c. may permit rates that are lower than the costs of production.

d. would not be possible if the demand curve for electricity was a horizontal line.

e. all of the above.

18. A good signal that a regulatory commission was attempting to hold the rates charged by power companies at too low a level would be:

a. lack of complaints from customers.

b. rates that didn't change.

c. an expansion of service by the utility.

d. a rate of return to investors that was less than that available on other investment options.

e. rates that were equitable to all consumers.

19. An example of an industry that is an oligopoly is:
    a. telephone
    b. grain farming
    c. electricity
    d. automotive manufacturing
    e. cattle raising
20. Natural monopolies may exist when:
    a. costs of production are very high.
    b. fixed costs are heavy compared to variable costs.
    c. the lowest cost output is experienced at very large volumes.
    d. the requirements for capital equipment expenditures are very large.
    e. all of the above.

ANSWERS

Reviewing the Chapter
1. normal, economic
2. right
3. negative economic
4. one
5. makers
6. few, many
7. horizontal, vertical
8. brand names, advertising, social acceptability, style
9. monopoly control over an economic resource; high initial capital requirements; patents on products or processes; dealership arrangements
10. price discimination, tying contracts, interlocking directorates
11. conglomerate
12. supplied
13. economic, revenue
14. increases, decreases
15. quantity, quantity and price
16. public utility, power company
17. discrimination
18. the multiple rate schedule will capture more of the area under the demand curve
19. investors

Self-Evaluation Exercises and Applications
1. Demand and supply:
    a. demand shifts from D to D_1.

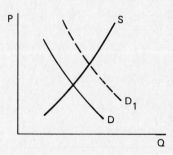

b. equilibrium price and quantity shift from P
    and Q to P_1 and Q_1.

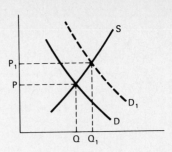

c. supply shifts from S to S_1.

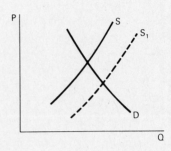

d. equilibrium price and quantity shift from P
    and Q to P_1 and Q_1.

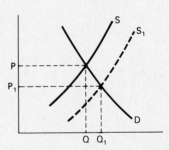

e. There won't be any economic profits because if there were, new firms would
    continue to be attracted to this business, increasing the supply, which lowers the
    price, until there were neither economic profits nor losses.

2. In monopoly:
    a. same as in question 1-a.
    b. same as in question 1-b.
    c. new firms can't enter the market if there is a monopoly, thus the relevant graph
        is still illustrated by 1-b.

d. same as answer 1-b.

e. economic profits can remain positive where there is monopoly power because new firms are not able to begin to produce the same product.

3. Lifeline electricity rates:

a. would encourage low-income families to use more electricity.

b. probably would cause an increase in the rates to other users so that the utility could regain the revenue lost by offering the lower rate to poor people.

c. might cause other users, such as industrial and commercial users, to respond to higher costs of electricity by raising the price of their product.

d. would discourage low-income families from practicing energy conservation.

e. are not a panacea for poverty. Low-income families are poor because they have less income than other groups of people, not because electrical rates are high. The problem of low incomes might be addressed more satisfactorily by a system of negative income taxes (see Chapter 12) or job-training programs.

f. might cause the rate of return on investment to decrease because lowered rates for one class of customer would result in less earnings for the utility. This is a problem when the utility has to finance new capital by selling bonds since the debt service costs on the bonds will be higher if the utility has lower earnings.

4. Total revenue = shaded area.

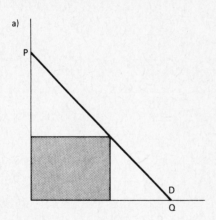
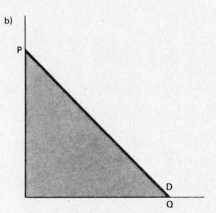

Chapter Test

True/False Questions

1. true	4. false	7. false	10. false
2. true	5. true	8. true	
3. false	6. false	9. false	

Multiple-Choice Questions

1. e; 2. c; 3. b; 4. e; 5. e; 6. b; 7. d; 8. e; 9. d; 10. e; 11. e; 12. a; 13. c; 14. b; 15. c; 16. a; 17. e; 18. d; 19. d; 20. e.

CHAPTER 5
Labor Markets and the Labor Movement

CAPSULE SUMMARY

This chapter uses the demand and supply tools developed in Chapters 2 and 3 to analyze the productive resource known as *labor*. The equilibrium price is the wage rate, and the equilibrium quantity is the level of employment.

Not all labor markets work as if they were competitive. Restrictions on labor supply and nonequilibrium prices are often imposed by labor unions.

Reasons for shifts in the supply and demand curves for labor are examined. Some of these include the increased productivity of labor, the value of leisure time, sectoral shifts in product demand, and recessions. All of these shifts affect equilibrium wages and employment levels.

REVIEWING THE CHAPTER

1. Division of labor implies that each worker _____ in the production of a single good, or a part of that good. (86)

2. Fixed resources are those that can't be _____ in quantity in the short run. _____ resources are easily increased or decreased in both the short- and long-run time periods. (88)

3. Continuing to add variable resources to a fixed plant will result in _____ returns from each extra unit of the variable resource. (88)

4. If the value of Mr. Hayes' output is $10, and his wage is $11, he _____ (should, should not) be hired. (87)

5. The demand for the services that labor can produce is _____ from the demand for the product that labor produces. (90)

6. The demand curve for a productive resource slopes downward because _____

_____

_____. (87, 88)

7. The upward sloping supply curve for a productive resource reflects the fact that

_____

_____. (87)

8. Many writers, such as Karl Marx, have described the unequal power between the

   workers and the _____ and believed that eventually the workers

   would revolt and _____ would be the result. (91)

9. The union movement grew substantially during the Industrial _____

   in Europe. (91–92)

10. Craft unions restrict membership to those _____

    _____,

    whereas _____ unions accept all workers as members who are

    employed in a particular industry. (92)

11. _____ boycotts are refusals of a union to work in a firm because of

    that firm's policies toward another union and are _____ (legal, il-

    legal). (93)

12. Many southern states have _____-to-work laws that make com-

    pulsory union membership illegal. (93)

13. Unionism today involves approximately _____ (one fifth, one third,

    one half, two thirds) of the labor force, and this is a/an _____

    (decrease, increase) when compared with 30 years ago. (93)

14. A backward-bending supply curve implies
    that at some fairly high wage rate, most
    workers would prefer more

    _____ to more

    _____. (98)

    Sketch a backward-bending supply curve
    on the graph to the right. Indicate how

Wage

Q

high your wage would have to be to keep you from working more for greater income.

15. If a union is successful at restricting entry of new workers into a particular line of work, wages will be _____ (higher, the same as, lower) than without the union. (99)

16. If union and management do not agree on wages or other conditions of employment, the workers may threaten to _____. (99)

17. Administered pricing has helped wages increase because it is easy for those firms with pricing power to pass on the higher _____ of production to the consumer. (100)

18. Unions have the greatest bargaining power when there are _____ (few, many) substitute workers for their union members. (100)

19. When an arbitrator enters into a union–management conflict, the arbitrator's decision is _____ on both the union and management for the length of the contract. (101)

20. Industries that are more _____ intensive have experienced greater increases in productivity than those industries that are relatively _____ intensive. (102)

SELF-EVALUATION EXERCISES AND APPLICATIONS

1. The American Bar Association, along with the associations of other professions, provides state-by-state testing of applications for permission to practice law in each state. Graduate lawyers must take an examination, written and graded by lawyers of the state where they want to practice, that if passed, allows them admission to that state's bar. If you were a lawyer who had a practice in New York, how anxious would you be to have new lawyers pass the N.Y. bar exam? Is there any similarity between this situation and that of craft unions? Use demand and supply curves to illustrate.

2. Many states are competing to have new business locate within their borders. Some of the things that firms look for in making locational decisions are energy costs, climate, access to markets, labor costs, transportation systems, and tax structure. If you ran a state economic development department, which of these could you change to encourage more development? What effect would right-to-work laws have?

3. Recent demographic changes have indicated that the birth rate in the U.S. has fallen. How will that affect the demand and supply of public school teachers? Compare the effects both five and ten years from now.

4. The Organization of Petroleum Exporting Countries (OPEC) can restrict the supply of oil available to the U.S. How will this affect:
   a. the production of products using oil.

   b. the production of automobiles.

   c. the price of oil.

   d. the exploration for substitute energy sources.

   e. the demand for domestic oil.

CHAPTER TEST

True/False Questions

T F 1. It is possible that by continuing to add variable resources to a given quantity of fixed resources, the extra output from the last unit of variable resources could be negative.

T F 2. Worker alienation refers to the situation in which workers are performing simple and unchallenging tasks and become mentally separated from their work product.

T F 3. The pay that each worker receives will approximate the value of the extra output that he produces.

T F 4. Labor receives a greater proportion of the national income than any of the four types of productive resources.

T F 5. A backward-bending supply curve of labor assumes that, at some high wage, the number of hours worked will decrease and so will income.

T F 6. One problem that unions have caused for their members is to push some wages so high that consumers discover substitute products, and the derived demand for the union workers decreases.

T F 7. In a unionized firm, the workers who have the longest employment records will also usually have the greatest job security.

T F 8. If a firm has to invest a great deal of resources into meeting environmental and safety standards, the productivity of that firm will tend to grow more rapidly than one that didn't have to meet those standards.

T F 9. Decreases in productivity are likely to worsen inflationary pressures.

T F 10. Collective bargaining always results in a contract that is agreeable to both the union and the management.

Multiple-Choice Questions

1. It is possible to increase production by:
   a. adding more fixed resources.
   b. adding more variable resources.
   c. adding more fixed and variable resources.
   d. using more fixed resources more intensively.
   e. all of the above will increase production.

2. The optimum quantity of resources to be hired is:
   a. where the value of the extra output from that resource is barely greater than the cost of hiring that resource.
   b. where the value of the extra output from that resource is greater than the cost of hiring that resource.
   c. where the value of the extra output from that resource is higher than the minimum wage.
   d. where the value of the extra output from that resource is profitable.
   e. none of the above.

3. Labor union growth has been encouraged by:
   a. economic prosperity.
   b. high wages.

    c. the Taft-Hartley Act of 1947.

    d. the decrease in employment in manufacturing relative to the service industries.

    e. President Roosevelt's Wagner National Labor Relations Act.

4. A union shop is legal and:

    a. requires that employers hire only union members.

    b. requires that workers join a union after they are hired.

    c. requires that people refuse to do business with a unionized firm.

    d. is a "right-to-work" law.

    e. can operate as a secondary boycott.

5. As the supply of elementary school teachers increases, assuming no other changes, the following will probably occur:

    a. the price for those teachers will increase.

    b. the price for those teachers will decrease.

    c. the demand for the teachers will increase.

    d. the quantity demanded of teachers will increase.

    e. both b and d are correct.

6. If labor unions effectively restrict the supply of workers to a particular firm:

    a. the price will increase.

    b. the quantity demanded will decrease.

    c. more workers will try to join those unions.

    d. the supply curve of those workers becomes vertical at the union wage rate.

    e. all of the above.

7. Rising wages in the U.S. are probably *not* the result of:

    a. high employment levels.

    b. administered pricing by monopolies.

    c. union pressures.

    d. excess labor supply.

    e. increased labor productivity in the U.S.

8. Future increases in productivity are *not* likely to be as great as past increases because:

    a. new entrants to the labor market are highly skilled ones.

    b. the proportion of income spent on services is growing, relative to goods.

    c. industry is becoming more capital intensive.

    d. environmental legislation is changing the quality of capital.

    e. none of the above.

9. Benefits from having workers become part owners of the firms in which they work include:

    a. increased workers' wage demands.

    b. a less equal distribution of income.

    c. the fact that workers will try to run the firms, and since they're not trained to make management decisions, output may fall.

    d. greater commitment to producing a better product.

    e. greater use of workers' councils.

10. Unions are typically concerned with improving:

    a. pensions.   d. working conditions.

    b. hours.   e. all of the above.

    c. salaries.

11. Specialization of function in labor markets allows:
    a. self-sufficiency in production.
    b. greater output than if each worker produced the complete good.
    c. longer work hours.
    d. the production of services rather than goods.
    e. a backward-bending supply curve of labor.
12. The demand curve for labor slopes downward and to the right because:
    a. more workers will be hired at lower wages.
    b. of the law of variable proportions.
    c. after some point, each extra worker adds less to total output than the previous worker hired.
    d. very high wage rates will encourage employers to substitute other resources for labor.
    e. all of the above.
13. Labor's share of total output of our economy has increased due to:
    a. the increasing capital intensiveness of the production process.
    b. the reduced importance of labor unions.
    c. rapidly increasing price levels.
    d. the improved quality of the labor force.
    e. the trend of workers returning to self-employment.
14. The greatest real wage gains have been evident in:
    a. metal, oil, and tobacco production.
    b. mining and construction.
    c. printing and publishing.
    d. furniture and clothing.
    e. finance and real estate.
15. Karl Marx stressed the importance of:
    a. class conflict.
    b. the differences between property owners and nonowners.
    c. the eventual worker revolution.
    d. the exploitation of workers.
    e. all of the above.
16. Right-to-work laws:
    a. have been passed by most states.
    b. allow only union members to have jobs.
    c. restrict the supply of labor, thereby increasing wages for those hired.
    d. are allowed by the Wagner Act.
    e. forbid union shops.
17. A reduction in the available quantity of a resource will:
    a. cause a shift in the demand curve.
    b. cause a shift in the supply curve.
    c. reduce the price of the resource.
    d. cause a movement along a given supply curve.
    e. none of the above.
18. The supply curve of labor can bend backward:
    a. at low wages.

    b.   if the opportunity costs of working are very high.

    c.   if leisure has a low value.

    d.   if the worker wishes a higher standard of living.

    e.   if the quantity of other resources is reduced.

19.   If unions can efficiently restrict the supply of labor available to a particular market:

    a.   the supply curve of labor will shift to the left.

    b.   the equilibrium price of labor will increase.

    c.   there will be a movement along the demand curve.

    d.   the quantity of labor hired will be less than if the labor supply hadn't been reduced.

    e.   all of the above.

20.   Recessions might be expected to lower average wages because:

    a.   government has pursued policies that encourage full employment.

    b.   the supply of labor to industry from the shrinking private sector continues to shift the entire supply curve to the right.

    c.   the entire demand curve for labor would shift to the left.

    d.   inflation rates are less in recessions than in good economic times.

    e.   all of the above.

ANSWERS

Reviewing the Chapter

1. specializes
2. changed, variable, long
3. diminishing
4. should not
5. derived (generated)
6. the productivity of each additional unit of variable resource eventually falls as more variable resources are added to the fixed resources
7. a greater quantity will be offered at higher prices
8. capitalists, communism
9. Revolution
10. with a particular skill, industrial
11. secondary, illegal
12. right
13. one fifth, decrease
14. leisure, work (see figure 5.4 on page 98 of text)
15. higher
16. strike
17. costs
18. few
19. binding
20. capital, labor

Self-Evaluation Exercises and Applications

1. Entrance exams:

    If the supply curve of lawyers was S without the entrance exams, and some applicants failed the exams, the supply curve becomes S_1, raising the price of lawyers' services from P to P₁, and reducing the quantity of legal services demanded. Economic analysis shows that bar examinations and the craft unions restrict the supply of labor in exactly the same way.

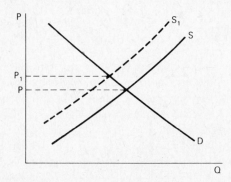

2. State economic development agencies can do little to change energy costs, climate, access to markets or transportation systems. They can, however, recommend the development of tax incentives for new and expanding business. In addition, the states with right-to-work laws have lower labor costs (not necessarily cause and effect) and a right-to-work law certainly gives business more options for hiring labor.

3. Falling birth rates now will reduce the demand for teachers, but that effect will not take place until the demographic changes are fully reflected in the school population.

4. A reduction in oil supply will:
   a. increase the price of products produced with oil.
   b. if availability of gasoline is restricted and price is increased, reduce the number of cars demanded and the number produced.
   c. increase the price of oil.
   d. encourage the exploration of substitute energy sources.
   e. increase the demand for domestic oil.

Chapter Test

True/False Questions

1. true	4. true	7. true	10. false
2. true	5. false	8. false	
3. false	6. true	9. true	

Multiple-Choice Questions

1. e; 2. a; 3. e; 4. b; 5. e; 6. e; 7. d; 8. b; 9. d; 10. e; 11. b; 12. e; 13. d; 14. a; 15. e; 16. e; 17. b; 18. b; 19. e; 20. c.

Measuring Economic Activity

CAPSULE SUMMARY

Before economists can analyze the way an economy performs, they must develop ways to measure the level of economic activity. Several methods are reviewed in Chapter 6.

The first is to use circular flow analysis, which looks at the sources and uses of resources and produced goods and the roles of households and firms.

The second way to measure the level of economic activity is to examine all the sources of aggregate demand in an economy and to compare total demand with the output supplies. Sources of demand included consumers, investors, and the government.

The final method is to compare the money value of output with a measure of the "real" value of that output. This method subtracts inflation's effects from GNP measures.

REVIEWING THE CHAPTER

1. Macroeconomics studies the total production of goods and services in all markets.

   This is in contrast to _____, which studies individual markets separately. (107)

2. The circular flow in the economy works in two directions. One flow, the

   _____ (money, real goods) one, follows the movement of real

   resources as inputs into business and the production of goods and services. The other

   flow, the _____ (money, real goods) one, follows the income earned

   through production used to purchase the output of businesses. (107)

3. The three major spending units in the economy are households who spend money for

   _____ goods, businesses who spend money for _____

   goods, and the government who spends money to finance its programs. (108)

4. Net exports is defined as _____

   _____

   _____. (108)

5. Gross national product figures are usually given for only _____

   (final, intermediate) goods and services. (109)

6. Gross national product measures the value of expenditures on output or aggregate

_____ and the value of the income earned by resources or aggregate

_____. (110)

7. When GNP grows at the same rate as the country's increase in productivity and

resources, the country is producing _____ (above, on, under) its pro-

duction possibility curve. (110)

8. A recession is experienced when the economy fails to grow for _____

(one, two, four) consecutive quarter(s) of the year. (110)

9. Increased spending by the government will result in increased aggregate

_____ and, if the economy is not at full employment, will also result

in increased aggregate _____ as businesses produce more to fulfill the

greater needs of government. (110–111)

10. Economists would be wise to _____ (always, sometimes, never) try

to increase the country's GNP. (110)

11. Decreases in aggregate demand will first be seen as a decrease in _____

(inventories, incomes, sales), next as an increase in _____ (inven-

tories, incomes, sales), next as a decrease in _____ (production, in-

vestment), which causes a decrease in _____ (incomes, government

spending), and a further decrease in _____ (inventories, sales,

government spending). (111)

12. If C + I + G exceeds C + S + T, the circular flow will _____

(contract, remain unchanged, expand), and if I + G exceeds S + T, the circular flow

will _____ (contract, remain unchanged, ex-

pand). (112)

13. A price index is defined as _____

_____

_____. (116)

14. If the consumer price index was 150, it would cost $_____ to buy what cost $1000 in the base year (i.e., that prices have risen by _____%. (116)

15. Using Table 6.2 and reviewing the economic performance of the years 1973–76, note that in 1974 both consumption and investment expenditures were lower than in 1973, yet _____ (consumption, investment) expenditures recovered to their previous levels more rapidly than did the _____ (consumption, investment) expenditures. (117)

16. Also using Table 6.2, note that _____ (money, real) GNP continued to increase during the 1974–75 recession, whereas _____ (money, real) GNP fell. This is due to the inflation rate being _____ (greater than, less than) the decrease in the _____ (money, real) GNP. (117)

17. The price index shown in Table 6.2 shows prices lower in 1933 and 1939 than they were in 1929 and 1945. What may have accounted for this price decrease? _____ _____ _____. (117)

18. _____ economic welfare is a measure of economic well-being that subtracts the costs of production borne by society from the more usual measure of welfare (GNP), which only deducts those costs of production borne by _____ firms. (118)

19. Requiring that all firms bear their complete costs of production (both private and social) would probably be _____ (less, more) inflationary than our current methods of dealing with these problems. (118)

20. In a recession government expenditures tend to _____ (fall, remain stable, increase). This is particularly true of the category called _____ _____. (119–120)

SELF-EVALUATION EXERCISES AND APPLICATIONS

1. Draw a circular flow diagram. Be sure to include businesses, households, government, investment, and real and money flows for incomes and expenditures, savings, and taxes.

2. Since 1968 the price level has more than doubled, with most of the increases occurring in the past five years. How might these price increases affect gross national product, consumer spending, business conditions, and the economy in general? (This subject will be addressed in more detail in Chapter 10.)

CHAPTER TEST

True/False Questions

T   F   1. Gross national product is the dollar value of all final goods and services produced for sale in one year.

T   F   2. Businesses do not pay all of their income to resources—they must also pay taxes and save some income.

T   F   3. When resources are unemployed, it can be said that an economy is operating inside its production possibility curve.

T   F   4. It is possible to produce at a point outside the production possibility curve, but this only happens when there is inflation.

T   F   5. Increased spending on investment goods will usually increase GNP.

T   F   6. A firm's first evidence of decreased sales is often an unexpected buildup of inventories.

T   F   7. If consumers do not spend all of their income, the circular flow will shrink, and aggregate demand will fall.

T   F   8. When inflows to the circular flow exactly balance the outflows, the entire economy is said to be in equilibrium.

T   F   9. Money GNP grows faster than real GNP when there is inflation.

T   F   10. The service industry is relatively labor intensive in comparison with manufactured goods.

Multiple-Choice Questions

1. Government transfer payments:
   a. are not included in the circular flow diagram.
   b. are used primarily to supplement citizens' incomes.

    c.   include veterans' benefits.

    d.   are not direct payments for goods and services.

    e.   all of the above are described by government transfer payments.

2. Not all of the proceeds from the sales of goods and services are paid directly to resources. Some proceeds that are *not* received by the land, labor, managers, and capital are:

    a.   business taxes.

    b.   profits.

    c.   the portion of the price of a good that represents inflation.

    d.   household savings.

    e.   national income.

3. Included in the gross national product calculations for 1981 are:

    a.   automobile body parts produced in 1980 and used in a car produced in 1981.

    b.   the selling price of the automobile produced and sold in 1981 that used the parts produced in 1980.

    c.   The difference between the value of the parts produced in 1980 and the selling price of the car sold in 1981.

    d.   the sale of a used car in 1981 that was produced in 1975.

    e.   the purchase price of a share of General Motors stock.

4. If aggregate demand increases:

    a.   the aggregate supply will also increase.

    b.   the circular flow will remain unchanged.

    c.   the increased aggregate demand will always cause inflation.

    d.   consumers must have decreased their savings relative to their consumption.

    e.   the level of spending must have increased.

5. Outflows from the circular flow include:

    a.   taxes and savings.

    b.   consumption and savings.

    c.   business investment and depreciation.

    d.   business investment and taxes.

    e.   government transfer payments.

6. Which of the following is *not* an example of external costs of production:

    a.   smoke from factories that requires more frequent painting of nearby houses.

    b.   sludge dumped into the ocean from an oil tanker.

    c.   hot water returned to a stream that was used to cool machinery but now kills fish.

    d.   hills stripped of vegetation by strip-mining operations.

    e.   scrubbers bought to clean the air emitted when coal is burned.

7. Which of the following is *not* a true statement:

    a.   consumption expenditures are the largest component of aggregate demand.

    b.   personal savings are more than 10% of income.

    c.   government purchases exceed government transfers.

    d.   wage and salary income is more than 70% of total income.

    e.   rental income is the smallest of the four major categories of income earned by resources.

8. Which of the following is *not* characteristic of current government expenditures:

    a.   they represent approximately one third of GNP.

    b.   they have grown as a proportion of GNP in the past twenty years.

c. government transfers have grown more rapidly in the past few years than have government purchases of goods and services.

d. the growth of government transfer payments has been primarily due to government payments to finance wars.

e. as the proportion of government expenditures to GNP increase, the proportion of private expenditures to GNP must increase.

9. The percentage of consumer spending in which of the following categories has decreased since WW II:

a. nondurable goods.   d. services.

b. gasoline.   e. recreation.

c. automobiles.

10. The relative growth of the service sector is attributable to:

a. government aid for medical services.

b. the purchase of household services, perhaps due to the increased labor-force participation of females.

c. earlier retirement encouraging more spending on recreation and leisure.

d. the relative decrease in the size of the goods sector.

e. all of the above have contributed.

11. Money flows from business to households in the form of:

a. consumer spending.

b. C + I + G.

c. rents, wages, interest, and profits.

d. purchases of goods and services.

e. land, labor, capital, and entrepreneurship.

12. Income earned by productive resources is also called:

a. personal income.   d. total output.

b. disposable income.   e. national income.

c. gross national product.

13. A recession is technically defined as:

a. no growth in GNP (adjusted for inflation) for two consecutive quarters.

b. increased unemployment.

c. a position inside the production possibilities curve.

d. a reduction in aggregate supply.

e. a reduction in aggregate demand.

14. When aggregate demand increases:

a. the circular flow expands.

b. employment increases.

c. production is greater.

d. spending by consumers, investors, or the government increases.

e. all of the above.

15. Total spending in the economy may fall if:

a. consumers save less.

b. government increases its defense purchases.

c. taxes are lowered.

d. investors expect growth in consumer demand.

e. consumers fear a loss of jobs.

16. The total of tax rates of all levels of government tax are approximately what percentage of GNP:
    a. 10.   d. 40.
    b. 25.   e. 50.
    c. 35.
17. Net economic welfare (NEW) is different from GNP in that:
    a. changes in price levels are eliminated.
    b. only "good" goods are counted, and "bad" goods are subtracted.
    c. firms are forced to pay for their external costs with the NEW measure.
    d. taxes are subtracted from GNP.
    e. there is double counting of private costs in GNP.
18. Which of the following is the proportion of government spending contributed by state and local governments compared with the federal government:
    a. state and local 62%, federal 38%.
    b. state and local 50%, federal 50%.
    c. state and local 38%, federal 62%.
    d. state and local 20%, federal 80%.
    e. state and local 15%, federal 85%.
19. Which of the following statements does *not* depict an accurate trend in consumer spending? The proportion of income:
    a. devoted to services has increased.
    b. devoted to recreational spending has increased.
    c. devoted to spending for necessities has increased.
    d. devoted to spending for durables has increased.
    e. devoted to savings has increased.
20. As the service sector in our economy has grown:
    a. production has become more labor intensive.
    b. productivity gains have been slower.
    c. labor supply has shifted from manufacturing to service industries.
    d. jobs have become less routine.
    e. all of the above.

ANSWERS

Reviewing the Chapter
1. microeconomics
2. real goods, money
3. consumer, investment
4. the value of American goods purchased by foreigners minus the value of foreign goods that we buy
5. final
6. demand, supply
7. on
8. two
9. demand, supply
10. sometimes

11. sales, inventories, production incomes, sales
12. expand, expand
13. a percentage comparison of current prices to prices in a base year
14. 1500, 50
15. consumption, investment
16. money, real, greater than, real
17. significantly lower real output, a recession or depression
18. net, private
19. more
20. increase, transfer payments

Self-Evaluation Exercises and Applications

1. See text, Figures 6.1 and 6.2.
2. Price-level increases increase gross national product since this is a measure of the quantity of goods produced *times* their prices. Rapid price increases can encourage heavy debt commitments by consumers and businesses since the debt will be repaid with cheaper dollars and because the consumers and businesses think that they can save money by buying products and resources now rather than later when the prices are higher. Usually this increase in the faster spending rate can't be maintained for a long time, spending slows down, and business output decreases, often resulting in a recession.

Chapter Test

True/False Questions

1. true	4. false	7. false	10. true
2. true	5. true	8. true	
3. true	6. true	9. true	

Multiple-Choice Questions

1. e; 2. a; 3. c; 4. e; 5. a; 6. e; 7. b; 8. d; 9. a; 10. e; 11. c; 12. e; 13. a; 14. e; 15. e; 16. c; 17. b; 18. a; 19. c; 20. e.

CHAPTER 7

Cycles in Economic Activity

CAPSULE SUMMARY

This chapter uses the measures of economic activity developed in Chapter 6 to model a graphic presentation of an economy. Consumption, investment, and government spending, which are the components of aggregate demand, are combined with aggregate supply to illustrate the equilibrium level of income that will be generated by an economy.

This income level is compared with efficient, or ideal, income levels with respect to employment and inflation. When the ideal and efficient incomes are not the same, inflationary or deflationary gaps occur.

Productivity, as a means of increasing aggregate supply, is reviewed. A brief history of recent business cycles is presented.

Emphasis in this chapter is placed on becoming familiar with those analytical tools that will help you study the monetary and fiscal policies available to the government for altering equilibrium income. These policies are described in Chapters 8 and 9.

REVIEWING THE CHAPTER

1. Ideally, GNP should grow as rapidly as the increase in the _____ of a country's resources. (125–126)

2. Increases in the level of economic activity, followed by decreases, are known as _____. (126)

3. If aggregate demand exceeds aggregate _____, equilibrium GNP will _____. (128–129)

4. The change referred to in question 3 would be beneficial if resources were _____ and prices were relatively stable. (129)

5. The marginal propensity to consume compares a change in income with the increased _____ caused by that income change. (126)

6. If the MPC is 4/5, this means that $80 of every additional $100 of income is _____. (126)

7. The 45° line on the diagram below connects all the points where _____ is equal to _____. (128)

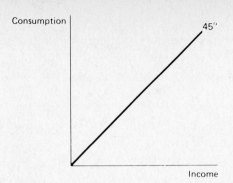

Consumption

45"

Income

8. Business investment is assumed _____ (to, not to) change as the level of income increases; thus the investment line is shown by adding a line _____ to the consumption function. (128)

9. Government expenditures _____ (do, do not) change as the level of income increases. This is because the size of government programs are dependent on _____. (128)

10. When aggregate demand is less than aggregate supply, the economy is operating at an income level _____ (higher, lower) than equilibrium. (128)

11. The level of demand described in question 9 will leave business with _____ (excess, deficit) inventories, and business will _____ (decrease, increase) the level of production, which will _____ (raise, lower) national income. (129)

12. Decreases in the level of government spending will _____ the equilibrium level of income. (131–132)

13. When aggregate demand (people's attempts to spend) exceeds production, the economy is said to have a/an _____ (inflationary, deflationary) gap. (131)

14. A decrease in spending (e.g., investment) causes a decrease in _____, which _____ (exceeds, is less than) the downward shift in investment by the _____ times the decline in investment. (132)

15. The size of the inflationary or deflationary gap is equal to the _____

    _____ necessary to close that gap. (132)

16. Why don't economic expansions continue indefinitely?

    _____

    _____

    _____. (131–132)

17. What sets the floor to a business cycle (i.e., why don't business downturns continue

    indefinitely)? _____

    _____. (132)

18. The most volatile (rapidly changing) component of aggregate demand is

    _____. (136)

19. The primary reason that the aggregate supply curve (plotted as quantity of output at

    different levels on a price index) begins to slope upward is that _____

    _____. (138)

20. U.S. productivity has _____ (declined, increased) in the late 1970s.

    (139)

SELF-EVALUATION EXERCISES AND APPLICATIONS

1. Draw a 45° line on the following graph. All points along this line represent points
   where spending is equal to _____.

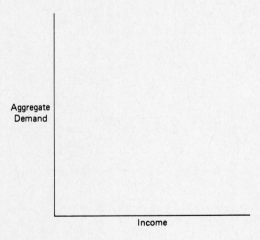

Expenditures
(Aggregate
Demand)

Income

Now sketch a typical consumption function on this diagram. Finally, sketch typical investment and government expenditure curves, and add these to the consumption function to illustrate aggregate demand.

2. Draw a 45° line (aggregate supply) and a typical aggregate demand curve (C + I + G) on the following graph. Define a level of income at which there would be a deflationary gap.

Aggregate
Demand

Income

3. On the following graph, sketch the relationship between aggregate demand and aggregate supply if the axes of the graph are redefined as an index of prices and quantity of output. What will happen to the price level (as measured by the price index) if aggregate demand increases? Show on the original graph.

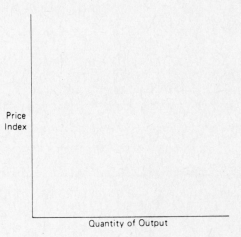

Price
Index

Quantity of Output

4. Now draw another identical set of aggregate supply and demand curves when the aggregate supply curve is flatter. How would you compare the difference in price response when demand increases?

Price
Index

Quantity of Output

When is the supply curve likely to be very steep?

CHAPTER TEST

True/False Questions

T   F   1. Stability in income can only exist at equilibrium.
T   F   2. A stable GNP would be a desirable goal for our economy.
T   F   3. The typical business cycle expands or contracts indefinitely.

T   F   4. Consumption expenditures exceed those for investment and by government.

T   F   5. The marginal propensity to consume can exceed unity (1) if spending is financed from borrowing or past savings.

T   F   6. If government expenditure increased by $25 B and the multiplier was 4, equilibrium income would increase by $100 B. This relationship implies an MPC of ¾.

T   F   7. A deflationary gap implies that the total demand for goods and services in an economy exceeds the productive capacity of that economy.

T   F   8. The larger the multiplier, the more susceptible the economy is to wide fluctuations in economic activity.

T   F   9. Recessions have occurred in the U.S. every two years, on average, since World War II.

T   F   10. If there is a great deal of excess productive capacity, the supply curve plotting the quantity of output on a graph with an index of prices will be very steep.

Multiple-Choice Questions

1. If the marginal propensity to consume is equal to 3/5:
   a. 60% of any increase in income will be consumed.
   b. if income increases by $500, savings will be increased by $200.
   c. an increase in aggregate demand of $100 will result in an increase in equilibrium income of more than $100.
   d. $15 of every $25 increase in income will be spent.
   e. all of the above will apply.

2. When aggregate demand is greater than aggregate supply at the target level of income, it might be desirable to:
   a. raise aggregate demand.
   b. raise the level of income.
   c. lower government spending or investment.
   d. raise consumption expenditures.
   e. increase the marginal propensity to consume.

3. If the sunspot theory of business cycles were correct:
   a. farm income would be the most important determinant of national income.
   b. sunspots would cause increases in the MPC.
   c. agricultural output would be determined by changes in manufacturing income.
   d. sunspots darken the sky and thus prevent crops from growing.
   e. none of the above would apply.

4. A business cycle can be defined as:
   a. recurrent increases and decreases in the level of economic activity.
   b. long-term economic growth.
   c. a depression.
   d. an increase in output per man hour.
   e. a steadily declining economy.

5. Once an increase in an expenditure takes place, it will:
   a. shift the aggregate demand curve upward.

b. result in a greater change in the level of income than the initial increase in expenditure.

c. result in a chain of additional increases in expenditure.

d. all of the above.

e. none of the above.

6. When aggregate demand and aggregate supply are plotted as a function of the price level as in the diagram to the right:

a. a decrease in expenditure shifts the aggregate supply curve to the left.

b. an increase in expenditure shifts the aggregate demand curve to the right.

c. an increase in aggregate supply increases the price level.

d. a decrease in aggregate supply lowers the price level.

e. an increase in aggregate demand always raises the quantity of goods and services produced.

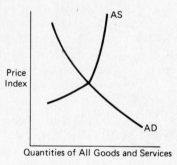

Quantities of All Goods and Services

7. If the aggregate supply curve is flat (horizontal):

a. the aggregate demand curve will determine the price level.

b. an increase in aggregate demand will increase prices.

c. the economy must be at full employment.

d. the economy must be in a recession.

e. larger quantities of goods will be supplied at constant prices.

8. Historically, recessions have usually followed:

a. decreases in employment levels.

b. adjustments in labor-force participation rates.

c. prolonged periods of peace.

d. periods of unusually heavy spending.

e. periods of unusually light spending.

9. The multiplier effect shows that:

a. when demand increases, there will be a larger increase in income.

b. when demand decreases, there will be a larger decrease in income.

c. income will increase as the level of government spending increases.

d. income will decrease when the level of investment decreases.

e. all of the above apply.

10. If a country's productivity increases at 5% per year, this means that:

a. there are 5% more workers every year.

b. there are no additional workers, but each one produces 5% more output per hour.

c. spending must increase at 5% per year so that unemployment rates don't increase.

d. there are 5% more machines every year.

e. all of the above are possibilities.

11. Unwanted inventory depletion at stores is a strong indicator that:
    a. aggregate demand has increased.
    b. aggregate demand has decreased.
    c. aggregate supply has increased.
    d. aggregate supply has decreased.
    e. none of the above.

12. The ideal level of growth in an economy is where the increase in the production of goods and services:
    a. is zero, that is, there is no growth.
    b. is rapid enough to fully employ all the resources available.
    c. equals the increase in the productive capacity of available resources.
    d. leads to unchanging prices.
    e. is not irregular.

13. An individual's MPC can exceed 1 if:
    a. there is full employment.
    b. there are transfer payments.
    c. the individual doesn't pay taxes.
    d. the individual's savings are growing.
    e. the individual borrows.

14. Investment and government spending:
    a. increase as income increases.
    b. fall as income increases.
    c. are graphed as if they were independent of the level of income.
    d. are graphed with exactly the same relation to income as consumer spending.
    e. together equal aggregate demand.

15. If equilibrium income equals $2 trillion and production equals $1.8 trillion:
    a. C + I + G is greater than output.
    b. inventories will have to be used to support a portion of sales.
    c. production will tend to increase.
    d. aggregate demand will exceed aggregate supply.
    e. all of the above.

16. Equilibrium income:
    a. is efficient.
    b. is on the production possibilities curve.
    c. will generate full employment.
    d. is inflationary.
    e. none of the above.

17. Recessions are characterized by:
    a. high unemployment levels.
    b. little inflation.
    c. increasing consumption spending.
    d. large purchases of consumer durables.
    e. reductions of business inventories.

18. The recession of 1980 was a short and sharp decline in economic activity. The one in 1981 was longer and:
    a. less severe.

b.　occurred during a period of greater inflation.

c.　entirely in the construction sector.

d.　a result of President Reagan's economic policies.

e.　none of the above.

19.　An increase in aggregate demand is possible without causing higher prices if:

a.　increases in output are always accompanied by increases in costs.

b.　the economy is close to full employment.

c.　the rate of inflation is falling.

d.　there are no unemployed resources.

e.　the aggregate supply curve is flat.

20.　Decreases in productivity can be caused by:

a.　increases in worker incentives.

b.　large infusions of workers into the labor force for first jobs.

c.　movement of labor out of agriculture.

d.　lower energy costs.

e.　none of the above.

ANSWERS

Reviewing the Chapter

1.　productivity
2.　business cycles
3.　supply, increase
4.　unemployed
5.　spending (consumption)
6.　consumed (spent)
7.　income, consumption
8.　not to, parallel
9.　do not, the public's need for government services
10.　higher
11.　excess, decrease, lower
12.　decrease
13.　inflationary
14.　income, exceeds, multiplier
15.　change in expenditures
16.　there is a finite limit to the quantity of resources available; shortages develop; and there is a decrease in the rate of increases of sales
17.　old plants and equipment wear out and are replaced, which increases aggregate demand
18.　investment
19.　resources become fully employed, thus to increase production, firms must pay higher prices to bid resources away from their present uses
20.　declined

Self-Evaluation Exercises and Applications

1.　Income:

All points on the 45° line represent equal spending and income.

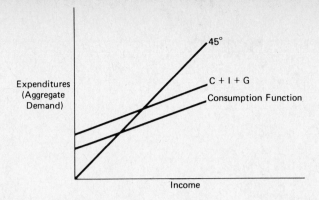

2. Equilibrium:

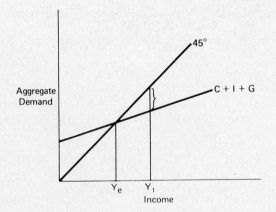

Y_e = equilibrium income.

Y_1 = full employment income if there's a deflationary gap. At Y_1 aggregate supply exceeds aggregate demand by the quantity in the bracket.

3. Aggregate demand and supply:

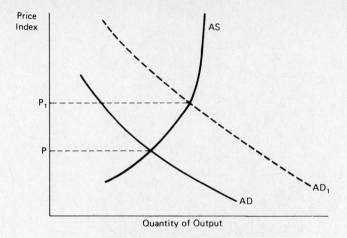

An increase in aggregate demand to AD_1 will cause the price index to increase from P to P_1.

4. Flatter aggregate supply:

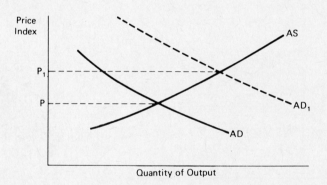

The increase in the price index will be less when the aggregate supply curve is flatter. The supply curve is likely to be very steep at full employment.

Chapter Test

True/False Questions

1. true	4. true	7. false	10. false
2. false	5. true	8. true	
3. false	6. true	9. false	

Multiple-Choice Questions

1. e; 2. c; 3. a; 4. a; 5. d; 6. b; 7. e; 8. d; 9. e; 10. e; 11. a; 12. c;
13. e; 14. c; 15. e; 16. e; 17. a; 18. a; 19. e; 20. b.

CHAPTER 8
Government Finance and Fiscal Policy

CAPSULE SUMMARY

Fiscal policy is one of the two major tools for influencing the size of consumption, investment, and government expenditures. The tools of fiscal policy, changes in taxes and changes in government expenditures, are reviewed, and their impact on equilibrium income is examined.

The public debt is created when government spending exceeds government receipts. The benefits and problems associated with the government debt are discussed, and the means of funding the debt are analyzed.

The chapter ends with a historical review of how fiscal policy has been used, and makes some projections for the future.

REVIEWING THE CHAPTER

1. Defense expenditures consume approximately _____ (one quarter, one half) of the federal budget, and income support payments represent _____ (one quarter, one third) of the budget. (144–145)

2. The most serious danger that occurs when the government prints new money is _____. (145)

3. One means of funding government expenditures is to borrow from the public. This is also known as _____ finance. (145, 146)

4. A _____ (regressive, progressive) tax is one that takes a larger percentage of income base from high-income earners than from low-income earners. (146–147)

5. The government taxes its citizens but returns some of those tax payments in the form of _____ payments. (147)

6. Low-income families are likely to pay _____ (lower, higher) tax rates than high-income families. They are also likely to receive _____ (lower, higher) transfer payments than high-income families, resulting in a

_____ (less, more) progressive net tax structure than if only the actual tax payments by families were considered. (147)

7. The tax-law changes in 1978 decreased the rate of taxation on capital gains. This legislation will probably make the personal income tax structure _____ (more, less) progressive. (147)

8. For taxpayers at most income levels, the total tax system, including all levels of government, is _____ (progressive, proportional, regressive). (147)

9. Welfare benefits are called an instrument of automatic fiscal policy because

_____. (148)

10. In times of noninflationary recession, tax payments _____ (decrease, increase) because taxpayers are taxed at _____ (lower, higher) tax rates, _____ (reducing, reinforcing) the decline in national income. (149–150)

11. New tax credits to stimulate investment in solar energy should be labeled as

_____ (monetary, fiscal) policy. (150)

12. _____ (Discretionary, Automatic) fiscal policy has an inflationary bias because politicians are usually more enthusiastic about increasing than decreasing government expenditures. (150)

13. The budgetary deficits that the federal government has seen in recent years have resulted in increases in the _____. (152)

14. The total public debt _____ (exceeds, is equal to, is less than) the size of the annual federal budget. (152)

15. Using budgetary deficits to offset decreases in private spending is an example of the use of a type of economic policy taught by _____. (154)

16. The argument that deficits are a result of high taxes suggests that _____ (private, public) expenditures will increase if tax rates are lowered. (154)

17. Presently the domestic unemployment rate is _____% and the rate of inflation is _____%. (158)

18. President Reagan's fiscal program is also referred to as _____

_____. (158)

19. Defense expenditures have _____ (increased,

remained constant, decreased) as a percentage of federal expenditures since World

War II. (159)

20. The main reason that the government sector cannot increase its productivity as rapid-

ly as the private sector is that the inputs for producing government services tend to be

more _____ (easily mechanized, labor inten-

sive) than those for the production of consumption and investment goods. (162)

SELF-EVALUATION EXERCISES AND APPLICATIONS

1. On the diagram that follows, show the effects of a fiscal policy that increases the
   equilibrium level of income in the following ways:
   a. by increasing government expenditures.
   b. by lowering taxes on consumers.

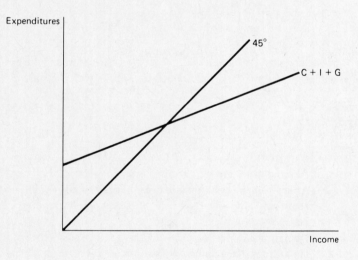

2. Describe the differences in the burden of the public debt if the debt were owned entirely by the citizens of the U.S. as compared with if the debt were owned entirely by foreigners.

3. The energy legislation that passed in the fall of 1978 and was endorsed by President Reagan included provisions to gradually decontrol the price of natural gas. On the following diagram label a price that would represent a ceiling price and a price that would prevail when there were no longer any controls. Compare the quantities demanded and supplied at the two prices.

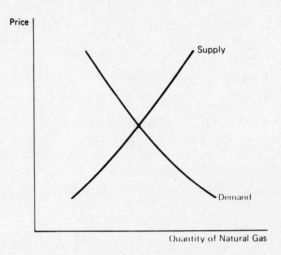

4. Describe the appropriate fiscal policies that could be followed if the economy was at full employment and the rate of inflation was considered too rapid.

CHAPTER TEST

True/False Questions

T   F   1. Negative taxes are a form of transfer payment.

T   F   2. An instrument of automatic fiscal policy is used to shift equilibrium income only after Congress recognizes that equilibrium income does not match the target level of income.

T   F   3. Discretionary fiscal policy would be a more satisfactory tool for managing aggregate demand if forecasting the level of economic activity in the future was a more exact science.

T   F   4. Deficit financing results in increases in national debt.

T   F   5. It will be necessary, at some time in the future, to completely repay the federal debt.

T   F   6. Many economists believe that the national debt does not put very much burden on the total citizenry of the future since some of those people are taxpayers and others are bondholders who receive the interest payments.

T   F   7. Most of our government bonds are held by foreigners rather than by our own citizens.

T   F   8. *Crowding out* refers to the phenomenon whereby extensive government borrowings increase the demand for loans, and thus push up interest rates, making it more expensive for the private sector to borrow and invest.

T   F   9. Holding the price of oil below equilibrium price in the U.S. will tend to encourage more consumption than would be the case at equilibrium price.

T   F   10. Future government expenditures are expected to grow more rapidly than future tax receipts primarily because inflation increases the cost of government services.

Multiple-Choice Questions

1. Revenue sharing is:
   a. taxes paid from current income by citizens.
   b. tax revenue collected at the state level and distributed by the federal government.
   c. tax revenue used to increase the fiscal drag.
   d. tax revenue distributed by the federal government to state and local governments.
   e. taxes paid that are used to pay off the public debt.

2. When the government finances its expenditures by printing new money:
   a. total spending will probably increase.
   b. consumer spending will probably not decrease.
   c. the supply of goods and services produced cannot increase if all resources are fully employed.
   d. there will probably be inflation.
   e. all of the above may happen.

3. Deficit finance may encourage:
   a. higher interest rates.
   b. lower interest rates.
   c. a smaller proportion of the federal budget paid out in interest expenses on the federal debt.
   d. greater private spending.
   e. businesses to pay lower taxes.

4. The most regressive tax of the following is:
   a. a tax on all sales and services.
   b. a tax on all sales.
   c. a tax on sales excluding food and drugs.
   d. a tax on savings.
   e. a tax on services.

5. An example of a progressive tax structure is:
   a. one that inceases the tax rates as incomes increase.
   b. most state and local tax structures.
   c. one that imposes the heaviest tax burdens on middle-income taxpayers.

d. one that is imposed to finance Social Security benefits.

6. Keynesian economics recommends:
   a. budgetary deficits when private spending is too low.
   b. budgetary surpluses when private spending is too low.
   c. budgetary deficits when there is an inflationary gap.
   d. budgetary surpluses when there is a deflationary gap.
   e. none of the above.

7. The following is *not* a good example of discretionary fiscal policy:
   a. the tax change in 1978 that decreased corporate income taxes from 48% to 46%.
   b. Congress's decision to increase defense spending.
   c. the sale of government bonds to banks.
   d. the increased unemployment benefits paid by the government during a recession.
   e. the decision to increase Social Security tax rates that took effect on January 1, 1979.

8. An example of contractionary fiscal policy is:
   a. a reduction in the money supply.
   b. a reduction in tax rates on businesses.
   c. an increase in government spending for the nation's infrastructure (e.g., railroads, bridges, highways, airports).
   d. an increase in Social Security payments to senior citizens.
   e. increases in personal income taxes.

9. Which of the following is *not* an incentive for the private sector to buy government bonds:
   a. interest income.
   b. a safe means of investment.
   c. a means of savings.
   d. a means of fully offsetting inflation.
   e. a way to help the government finance its spending.

10. The federal government collects approximately one quarter of the revenue spent by the state and local governments in our country because:
    a. state and local governments don't use income taxes.
    b. the federal government's tax structure generates greater revenue increases in times of increasing incomes than do those of state and local governments.
    c. state and local expenditures are usually more inefficient than federal expenditures.
    d. state and local governments have more needs than does the federal government.
    e. revenue-sharing programs have not been successful.

11. Most federal tax revenues are generated from:
    a. property taxes.
    b. gross receipts taxes.
    c. motor fuel taxes.
    d. sales taxes.
    e. corporate and personal income taxes.

12. Negative taxes:
    a. are paid as transfer payments to low-income families.
    b. must be subtracted from taxes collected to understand the impact of taxes on aggregate demand.
    c. when counted, increase the progressivity of the tax structure.

d.   add to the disposable income of certain groups in the economy.

e.   all of the above.

13.   When automatic stabilizers operate effectively they will:

a.   increase government transfers and tax levels when spending increases.

b.   produce an automatic surplus in the federal budget when spending increases too rapidly.

c.   produce an automatic deficit in the federal budget when spending increases too rapidly.

d.   reduce government transfers when other spending is reduced.

e.   reinforce any inflationary tendencies in an economy.

14.   Discretionary fiscal policy is said to have an expansionary bias because:

a.   voters are pleased when Congress cuts taxes.

b.   Congress finds it hard to reduce the size of programs that they have previously supported.

c.   tax increases are particularly painful to voters when there is a high level of inflation.

d.   economic stabilization policies have to be determined in a political environment.

e.   all of the above.

15.   Which of the following is not an advantage of the existence of a public debt:

a.   the debt helps finance deficit spending by the government.

b.   the debt provides a stabilization tool for the government.

c.   the debt is a safe investment option available for people in the U.S.

d.   the debt pays fairly high interest rates.

e.   the debt probably will never be repaid.

16.   Supply-side economics will reduce inflationary pressures if:

a.   it results in government spending increases.

b.   more output is produced.

c.   taxes are increased.

d.   incentives to save are diminished.

e.   the costs of borrowing for investment are increased.

17.   Reagan's economic program included:

a.   reducing the importance of the federal government sector as a percentage of GNP.

b.   cutting personal taxes, with the largest impact of the cuts on the rich.

c.   increasing defense spending.

d.   increasing business tax deductions, in order to increase after-tax earnings.

e.   all of the above.

18.   Legitimate criticisms of Reagan's economic program include:

a.   fear of large deficits.

b.   large tax reductions at low income levels, which will increase consumption.

c.   increases in defense spending, which is wasted output.

d.   reductions in government nondefense spending, which may lower the aggregate demand curve.

e.   none of the above.

19. If an economic program is planned with specific assumptions about the level of economic activity and those assumptions turn out to be overly optimistic with respect to tax revenues and the need for government transfers:
    a. equilibrium income will be higher than expected.
    b. employment will be higher than was planned.
    c. transfers will be lower than anticipated.
    d. the deficit will be larger than anticipated.
    e. economic growth will be greater than was expected.
20. When combining state, local, and federal taxes, it seems that the structure of taxes, taken as a whole:
    a. is proportional at most income levels.
    b. is progressive at most income levels.
    c. is regressive at most income levels.
    d. is regressive at high income levels.
    e. is progressive at low income levels.

ANSWERS

Reviewing the Chapter
1. one quarter, one third
2. inflation
3. deficit
4. progressive
5. transfer
6. lower, higher, less
7. less
8. proportional
9. as national income increases, the need for welfare payments decreases
10. decrease, lower, reducing
11. fiscal
12. discretionary
13. public debt
14. exceeds
15. Keynes
16. private
17. (adjust as necessary)
18. supply-side economics
19. decreased
20. labor intensive

Self-Evaluation Exercises and Applications

1. Fiscal policy:
   a) Expenditures

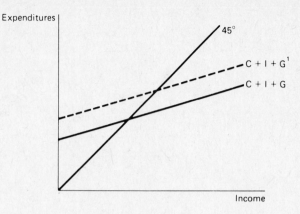

   b) Lowered consumption taxes

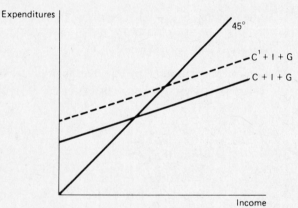

2. Debt owned by U.S. citizens represents income transfers when the debt is issued—from the debt purchasers to the recipients of the government payment—and when the debt is retired—from the taxpayers to the debt owners. However, if the debt is owned by foreigners, there will be an inflow of money to the U.S. when the debt is issued, and a loss of money when the debt is retired. The effects on economic activity will be larger when the debt is sold to foreigners.

3. Natural gas
   price decontrol:

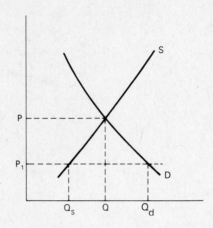

P₁ is a possible controlled price, Q_d would be the quantity demanded, and Q_s would be the quantity supplied. After decontrol, P would be the price, and the quantity demanded and supplied would be Q.

4. Contractionary fiscal policy would be appropriate policy, including increased taxes, budgetary surpluses, and decreased government spending.

Chapter Test

True/False Questions
1. true   4. false   7. false   10. false
2. false   5. false   8. true
3. true   6. true   9. true

Multiple-Choice Questions
1. d;   2. e;   3. a;   4. b;   5. a;   6. a;   7. d;   8. e;   9. d;   10. b;   11. e;   12. e;   13. b;
14. e;   15. e;   16. b;   17. e;   18. a;   19. d;   20. a.

CHAPTER 9

Banking and Monetary Policy

CAPSULE SUMMARY

The ability of the banking system to make loans and of the federal government to control the supply of money are the subjects of this chapter. Banks create money by lending excess reserves. The government influences the supply of money by (1) changing bank reserve requirements, (2) buying and selling bonds, and (3) setting the discount rate.

The accounting procedures employed to monitor bank policies are used to illustrate how an initial deposit of funds can initiate monetary expansion that exceeds the size of the original deposit. A money multiplier is developed, which is analogous to the expenditure multiplier developed in Chapter 7. Both multipliers show the effect of a shift in one variable (excess reserves and C + I + G expenditures) on another (new money and national income). The connections are the multipliers, and the size of the multipliers are inversely related to the reserve requirement and the MPS.

The success of monetary policies in the past twenty years is reviewed, and some theories for improving the use of monetary policies are examined.

REVIEWING THE CHAPTER

1. A double coincidence of wants was necessary for a successful _____

   system of exchange to work. (168)

2. A function of money whereby it is accepted as payment for goods and, in turn, can

   be used to buy goods and services is called _____. (169)

3. Characteristics of gold that allowed it to serve well as money were its

   _____ and _____. (169)

4. Member banks of the Federal Reserve System must purchase _____

   in the Federal Reserve Bank in their district and must keep a certain

   _____ of their deposits as reserves. (170)

5. Approximately _____ (4/5, 3/4, 1/2) of the country's money supply

   is under the control of the Federal Reserve System. (170)

6. The process of sorting checks and returning them to the bank where they were issued

   is called check _____. (170–171)

7. Money is defined as the sum of _____ and _____ held by the _____. (172)

8. Bank assets are those things that the bank _____ (owes, owns), and bank liabilities are those things that the bank _____ (owes, owns). (172)

9. When a bank accepts a deposit and then turns around and makes a _____ with a portion of that deposit, it has created money. (172)

10. The capital account of a bank must always represent the difference between the bank's assets and _____ since it represents the portion of total assets that would remain if all liabilities were paid. (173)

11. A single bank can only lend the amount of its _____ (excess, total, deficit) reserves, yet the banking system as a whole can lend _____ (its total, a multiple of the) excess reserves. (175)

12. The formula that shows the relation between newly created money and excess reserves is _____. (175)

13. When the loans that are repaid at a bank exceed the new loans extended, that bank has effectively _____ (increased, not affected, decreased) the available money supply. (176)

14. When the Federal Reserve uses open-market operations to _____ (expand, contract) the money supply, it should do so by buying bonds from the public. (178)

15. _____ increases in the money supply have often been suggested as an alternative to discretionary monetary policy. These increases could work toward economic stability if the rate of increase corresponded to the rate of increase in the country's _____. (179)

16. The equation used in the quantity theory of money describes the relation between total spending and the value of output. It states that money times _____ must equal _____ times the quantity of goods and services produced. (181)

17. A definition of money that includes time deposits is called _____. (182)

18. Even when excess reserves are plentiful and interest rates are low, the money supply will not increase unless banks are willing to make new _____. (183)

19. Traditionally, bank lending was based on its assets—when it needed more excess reserves it could sell bonds and switch the proceeds to its reserve account. Recently, bank lending has been based on its _____, whereby extra funds have been secured by offering interest incentives to customers to encourage increases in deposits. (186)

20. Banks are one of several types of _____ intermediaries. Others are _____ and _____. (186)

SELF-EVALUATION EXERCISES AND APPLICATIONS

1. Why do banks not have to physically keep all the money that has been deposited in them? What happens when all the depositors return for their money? How does this differ from the days when all the gold miners tried to withdraw their gold from the banks?

2. Trace the following transactions on these T-accounts (assume that the reserve requirement on demand deposits is 25%):

a. John takes $200 from his piggy bank and deposits that cash in his bank. In exchange he opens a checking account with a balance of $200.

John's Bank

Assets	Liabilities

b. John's bank sends this cash to the Federal Reserve, where it will earn interest in a reserve account.

John's Bank

Assets	Liabilities

c. Jean needs to borrow money and comes to John's bank for a loan. She borrows all the excess reserves held by the bank.

John's Bank

Assets	Liabilities

d. Jean now withdraws all the money she borrowed to buy new tires for her car. The tire dealer deposits the check in his bank.

Tire Dealer's Bank

Assets	Liabilities

3. In the late 1970s, two instruments of monetary policy were used in an attempt to convince the world that U.S. money had a stable value. Reserve requirements on deposits were increased, and the discount rate was raised. Describe how these policies should work, and whether or not they could achieve a stable value of U.S. currency.

4. Tight money policies are followed when the Fed wants to discourage business investments. Show the effects of a successful tight monetary policy on the C + I + G diagram that follows. Define the old equilibrium, the new equilibrium, and the probable target level of income.

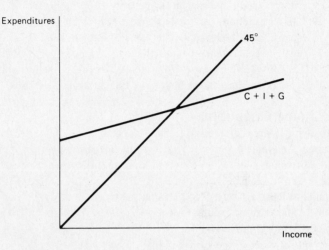

5. Assume that unemployment is the lowest it has been for five years, employment is the highest, and the economy is experiencing a 10% inflation. Describe an optimum monetary policy for this situation and justify your choice.

CHAPTER TEST

True/False Questions

T   F   1. A severe inflation undermines the ability of a monetary unit to serve as a store of value.

T   F   2. Most banks are Federal Reserve System members.

T   F   3. Near monies are generally more liquid than the more narrowly defined money.

T   F   4. The primary functions of commercial banks are to hold deposits for their customers and to regulate the supply of money.

T   F   5. An optimum monetary policy would be one where the money supply always remained unchanged.

T   F   6. If there aren't any excess reserves in the banking system, raising the reserve requirement will result in a decrease in the money supply that exceeds the increased reserves.

T   F   7. Easy money will include the following policies: lowering the discount rate, reducing the reserve requirement, and selling government bonds.

T   F   8. Contractionary monetary policy may not be successful in an inflation if borrowers continue to feel that the higher interest rates will be covered by higher prices and new investments will still be profitable.

T   F   9. In an inflation, real estate loans appear to be a good investment for a bank since the revenue from the real estate should be increasing and thus will be sufficient to pay off the loan.

T   F   10. Banks would be more likely to withdraw from membership in the Fed if the Fed required very high reserves held against deposits.

Multiple-Choice Questions

1. The following is/are the necessary function(s) of money:
   a. standard of value.
   b. store of value.
   c. medium of exchange.
   d. all of the above.
   e. none of the above.

2. The National Banking Act of 1863 was passed to:
   a. prevent banks from lending to foreigners.
   b. regulate state chartered banks.
   c. prevent increases in the money supply.
   d. require that all banks maintain 100% reserves against their deposits.
   e. regulate banks chartered by the federal government.

3. Which of the following is *not* true with respect to the Federal Reserve System:
   a. the seven-member Board of Governors is appointed by the President of the U.S.
   b. all banks are required to be members.
   c. Federal Reserve banks act as bankers for the U.S. Treasury.
   d. each member of the Board of Governors is appointed for a term of 14 years.
   e. there are 12 Federal Reserve districts.

4. Why do banks become members of the Federal Reserve:
   a. because they are federally chartered.
   b. because they can borrow from the Federal Reserve.
   c. because the Fed assists in their check-clearing operations.
   d. because their stock in the Fed earns dividends.
   e. all of the above.

5. The following are examples of bank assets:
   a. reserves held at the Fed.
   b. demand deposit accounts of customers.
   c. savings accounts of customers.
   d. vault cash.
   e. a and d are both bank assets.

6. The reserve requirement is 30%. If there are $500 excess reserves in the banking system, the maximum increase in the money supply that can be generated is:
   a. $1667.
   b. $1500.
   c. $500.
   d. $1000.
   e. none of the above is correct.

7. Expansionary monetary policy is most likely to result in increasing economic activity if:
   a. inflation rates are high.
   b. incomes are falling rapidly.
   c. businesses are anticipating a rapid growth of income.
   d. there are short time lags.
   e. interest rates have been very low for a long period of time.

8. High interest rates present more hardship to:
   a. home buyers than renters.
   b. creditors than debtors.
   c. large firms with internal sources of funds than consumers who buy those goods on credit.
   d. consumers who purchase durable goods with cash than consumers who buy those goods on credit.
   e. governments with no outstanding bonds than to governments with high levels of bonded indebtedness.

9. Arguments against discretionary monetary policy include:
   a. the long time lag between the policy action and when the policy takes effect.
   b. the possibility of monetary policy being used for political goals.
   c. the lack of perfect information upon which to base the discretionary changes.
   d. the differential impact that high and changing interest rates have on the various sectors of the economy.
   e. all of the above are arguments against discretionary monetary policy.

10. When would easy money result in higher interest rates?
    a. when the interest rates have reached the maximum heights that the government will allow.
    b. when the higher incomes generated by the easy money increase the demand for money to more than offset the increased supply.
    c. when M-1B grows faster than M-1A.
    d. if the economy was in a recession.
    e. if the velocity of money was decreasing.

11. Interest in bartering has increased in the early 1980s. One reason is that:
    a. tax rates have been reduced.
    b. discovering the "double coincidence of wants" has been made easier by computer technology.
    c. the IRS has imposed stricter enforcement procedures to tax the proceeds of a banker.
    d. inflation rates have been lowered.
    e. none of the above.

12. Since the Banking Act of 1980, all commercial banks must comply with Federal Reserve regulations. In exchange they benefit because:
    a. the Fed clears all their checks.
    b. they have to keep cash deposits at the Fed that do not earn interest.
    c. they have to buy stock in their Federal Reserve Bank.
    d. most banks are members of the Fed.
    e. they can more effectively compete with savings and loan institutions.

13. Credit unions are usually able to loan money at lower rates than other financial institutions because:
    a. they can attract more funds.
    b. their investments earn higher rates of return.
    c. their check-clearing costs are lower.
    d. they have fewer borrowers.
    e. the borrowers are less likely to default.

14. A bank can lend out:
    a. all of its reserves in excess of required reserves.
    b. all of its reserves.
    c. its required reserves.
    d. all of its assets.
    e. the reserves it maintains at the Fed.

15. Commercial banks can create money by:
    a. buying bonds.
    b. lending excess reserves.
    c. selling stock.
    d. reducing deposits.
    e. none of the above.

16. The Federal Reserve System can increase the money supply by:
    a. raising reserve requirements.
    b. buying bonds.
    c. following a tight money policy.
    d. raising the discount rate.
    e. all of the above.

17. Open market operations:
    a. occur daily.
    b. involve buying and selling bonds.
    c. are handled by the Federal Reserve Bank of New York.
    d. affect the reserve position of member banks.
    e. all of the above.

18. High interest rates are often the result of tight monetary policies designed to reduce inflation. However, these high rates may generate other problems, including:
    a. increases in the size of savings accounts to earn the high rates.
    b. a reduced money supply.
    c. an outflow of capital to foreign investments.
    d. lower costs for government borrowing.
    e. reduced business investment.

19. M-1A is a definition of money that includes:
    a. checking accounts plus cash held by the public.
    b. checking accounts plus cash held by the public and savings accounts.
    c. checking accounts plus cash held by the public and near monies.

d. checking accounts plus cash held by the public and other checkable deposits.

e. checking accounts plus cash held by the public and other checkable deposits and near monies.

20. High interest rates accompanied high inflation rates throughout the 1970s. Part of this can be explained by:

a. adjustments of interest rates to real rates.

b. relatively rapid growth of the money supply.

c. Gibson's paradox.

d. lenders' expectations that high inflation rates would continue.

e. all of the above.

ANSWERS

Reviewing the Chapter

1. barter
2. medium of exchange
3. scarcity, durability, portability
4. stock, proportion
5. 3/4
6. clearing
7. demand deposits, currency, public
8. owns, owes
9. loan
10. liabilities
11. excess, a multiple of the
12. created money = excess reserves $\times \dfrac{1}{\text{reserve requirement}}$
13. decreased
14. expand
15. automatic, production
16. velocity, price
17. M_2
18. loans
19. liabilities
20. financial, insurance companies, savings and loan associations, credit unions

Self-Evaluation Exercises and Applications

1. Banks do not have to physically keep all deposits since only a small proportion of deposits are withdrawn at a single time. If all depositors should return for all their money, the bank could borrow from other banks or from the Federal Reserve System. In earlier times, when all the gold miners tried to withdraw their gold, the banks would have to close since they had no place from which to borrow.

2. T-accounts:

John's Bank

a.

Assets			Liabilities		
Cash	+	$200	Demand Deposits	+	$200

b.

Cash	−	$200			
Reserves	+	200			

c.

Loans	+	$150	Demand Deposits	+	$150

Tire Dealer's Bank

d.

Reserves	+	$150	Demand Deposits	+	$150

3. Raising reserve requirements results in decreasing the free reserves available for loans. If there are not any free reserves in the banking system, the banks must reduce their loans. This tends to reduce the money supply and available credit. Raising the discount rate makes it more expensive for banks to borrow from the Federal Reserve. This results in banks wanting to maintain a tight reserve policy and would also tend to have a contractionary influence on the money supply. The Fed's objectives will be achieved if it is able to maintain slower rates of growth in the money supply than have occurred in the past five years and thus, constrain inflation.

4. Expenditures

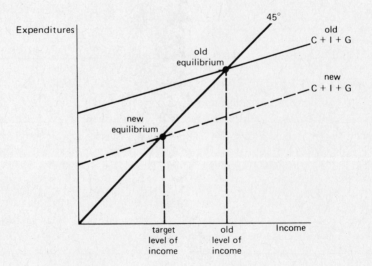

5. A "tight money" policy would probably be best for this situation. Holding back on increases in the money supply would (in theory) help to dampen inflationary pressures. At the same time, it would tend to increase unemployment; with employment at very high levels, however, it might be possible for the labor market to absorb some of the harmful employment effects of this policy.

Chapter Test

True/False Questions

1. true	4. false	7. false	10. true
2. false	5. false	8. true	
3. false	6. true	9. true	

Multiple-Choice Questions

1. d; 2. e; 3. b; 4. e; 5. e; 6. a; 7. c; 8. a; 9. e; 10. b; 11. b; 12. a; 13. e; 14. a; 15. b; 16. b; 17. e; 18. e; 19. a; 20. e.

CHAPTER 10

Inflation

CAPSULE SUMMARY

The inflation process is carefully analyzed in this chapter. Various theories as to the causes of inflation are reviewed. The problems that inflation presents are examined, and the history of recent attempts to control inflation are analyzed.

A case study on the U.S. experience with wage and price controls in the early 1970s is included. Study this carefully and try to determine the similarities and differences that exist between the inflation experience then and inflation in the early 1980s.

REVIEWING THE CHAPTER

1. When the average level of prices is increasing, there is _____. (193)

2. If velocity (V) doesn't change, and the supply of money (M) grows faster than the supply of goods (Q), _____ will rise, and inflation results. (194)

3. Assume that your family planned and saved for your college expenses in 1970, when price increases were averaging 3%, and invested their savings in a 5% savings account. Present rates of inflation are 8%. How has the change in inflation rates affected your family's ability to plan for the future? _____ _____. (195)

4. Producers who expect severe inflation may tend to _____ (increase, decrease) their stock of inventories since the prices of replacement supplies are likely to be higher than current prices. (195)

5. Many economists argue that slight inflation can be beneficial to the economy because it can _____ _____. (196)

6. Financing a war is possible by preventing the private sector from spending the money or by _____; by persuading the private sector not to spend the money

or by sales of _____; or by inflation, which is the same as the creation of new _____. (197)

7. Demand-pull inflation assumes that we are _____ (under, on) the production possibility curve. (196)

8. If inflation is caused by demand-pull elements in the economy, the federal government _____ (should, should not) be incurring deficits in its budget. (196)

9. If the money supply were to grow at a 4% rate, and production grew by 5% annually, the average level of prices would tend to _____ (fall, remain constant, rise). (197–198)

10. _____ inflation assumes that the initial blame for higher prices should be placed on the factors of production. (198)

11. The difficulty with stabilizing shares of incomes between the various types of resource owners (e.g., wages, rents, profits, and interest) is that _____

_____

_____. (199)

12. Increases in productivity are primarily the result of _____

_____. (199)

13. Price inflation accompanied by reduced production in industry is called

_____. (199)

14. Neither demand-pull nor cost-push can be a satisfactory explanation for inflation unless resources are _____ (unemployed, fully employed). (199)

15. _____ industries are those where the output of that industry is produced by only a few firms. There has been some indication that prices have risen _____ (more, as, less) rapidly in those concentrated industries. (199)

16. List several concentrated industries (i.e., those with a few large producers manufac-

turing the majority of a given product). _____
_____. (199)

17. The apparent connection between greater-than-average price increases in highly concentrated industries and the small number of these firms is a clue to the new inflation. List some of the structural factors in these industries that relate to this structural inflation. _____

_____

_____. (199)

18. The "Rule of _____" predicts the relation between a given rate of
inflation and the number of years that will pass before the value of money decreases
by 50%. (204)

19. If the rate of inflation is 7%, the value of the dollar will be cut in half in
_____ years. (204)

20. Federal government revenues increase more rapidly than the rate of inflation because

_____

_____

_____

_____. (205)

SELF-EVALUATION EXERCISES AND APPLICATIONS

1. President Carter announced a program of wage–price guidelines in November, 1978.
These included a maximum increase in wages of 7% and a limit on price increases to
1/2 percentage point less than the average of the previous two years. Carefully
describe the probable impact of such a plan on the economy.

2. How would optimum policies for dealing with inflation differ if there was:
   a. cost-push inflation?

   b. demand-pull inflation?

   c. stagflation?

   d. extensive monopoly?

   e. inflation accompanied by high rates of unemployment?

3. Use a demand and supply diagram to illustrate the effects of price controls that are below market equilibrium. What does your graph indicate about the probability of maintaining those controls over a long time period?

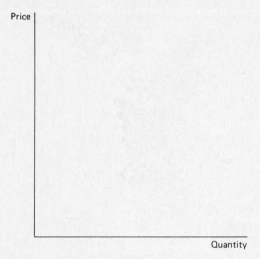

CHAPTER TEST

True/False Questions
T   F   1. A decrease in the average price level is called deflation.

T   F   2. Expectation of steadily increasing prices can be a self-fulfilling prophecy.

T   F   3. The most effective remedy to decrease demand-pull inflation is to cut total spending.

T   F   4. Milton Friedman believes that the optimum rate of growth in the money supply is the rate of growth of actual output.

T   F   5. Business firms frequently respond to cost-push inflation by increasing the prices of the goods that they sell.

T   F   6. Wages and salaries are a larger proportion of service-industry costs than they are of manufacturing-industry costs.

T   F   7. One typical guideline for administered prices is a target rate of return on investment.

T   F   8. The government probably suffers more than any other section from inflation since most of the services it provides are labor intensive and labor costs have been rising rapidly.

T   F   9. Most economists feel strongly that wage–price freezes cannot solve the underlying causes of inflation.

T   F   10. Government regulation is an anti-inflationary policy tool.

Multiple-Choice Questions

1. Free-trade theorists in the eighteenth century thought that any temporary imbalance between money and goods that caused inflation in one region would be automatically corrected by:
   a. encouraging those residents to sell more of their products in another region.
   b. encouraging other regions to purchase the first region's products, thus increasing the money supply in the first region.
   c. encouraging those residents to buy elsewhere, thus decreasing their money supply and correcting the imbalance.
   d. increases in the money supply to that region.
   e. none of the above.

2. The function of money that inflation interferes with is:
   a. store of value.
   b. medium of exchange.
   c. standard of value.
   d. all of the above.
   e. none of the above.

3. The group of people particularly hurt by inflation are:
   a. savers.
   b. retired folks living on fixed incomes.
   c. lenders.
   d. fixed income workers.
   e. all of the above.

4. Constant increases in the money supply at the same rate as increases in productive capacity would act to stabilize the economy because:
   a. when unemployment is high, the money supply would be growing at a faster rate than output, thus stimulating the economy.
   b. when inflation rates are high, the money supply would be growing at a faster rate than output, thus stimulating the economy.
   c. when unemployment is low, the money supply would be growing at a faster rate than output, thus stimulating the economy.
   d. when inflation rates are low, the money supply would be growing more slowly than the rate of inflation, thus causing economic contraction.
   e. none of the above.

5. Administered prices means that prices are:

a. automatically increased when the cost of living increases.

b. set by the federal government according to prescribed standards.

c. determined by national guideposts.

d. determined by the market forces of supply and demand.

e. set by large firms in a concentrated industry and followed by small firms.

6. Nixon's wage–price controls of 1971 were in response to:

a. inflation caused by excess demand.

b. pressures on the economy from the Vietnam War.

c. fear of inflation from expansionary fiscal policy.

d. a need to break the inflationary psychology.

e. all of the above.

7. Indexation helps to correct the distortions in relative prices caused by inflation and:

a. is used widely in the U.S. today.

b. would only apply to relative wage shares.

c. would prevent government revenues from taxation from growing more rapidly than income.

d. would cause the government's share of the economic pie to shrink.

e. would prevent stagflation.

8. The purpose of government regulation is to:

a. prevent bankruptcies of small businesses.

b. prevent the harmful effects of monopoly on the economy.

c. aid firms to produce at the most efficient level of output.

d. increase industrial concentration.

e. encourage growth of several firms in each industry.

9. Higher oil prices are the result of:

a. inflation.

b. increased demand for oil.

c. the greater costs of supplying new oil.

d. the lack of alternative sources of cheap energy.

e. all of the above.

10. The arguments against wage–price controls include:

a. the probable shortages that will occur.

b. the probable excess supply they will encourage.

c. the fact that they will be accompanied by a reduction in the money supply.

d. the probable reduction in demand that will occur.

e. their recent successes in holding down long-term inflation.

11. Which of the following is *not* a problem of unexpected inflation:

a. the stored value of money assets decreases.

b. those with fixed incomes are hurt.

c. past savings will buy less than had been planned.

d. lenders will be paid back in assets that may not compensate for the high inflation rates.

e. borrowers will have to pay back debts in currency that has gained purchasing power.

12. Milton Friedman advocates:

a. Keynesian aggregate demand theory.

b. constant 4% annual increases in the money supply.

c. raising productivity to deal with inflation.

d. wage and price controls.

e. reductions in union wages.

13. Stagflation is characterized by:

a. slow growth.

b. a low level of resource employment.

c. inflation.

d. none of the above.

e. all of the above.

14. Administered prices are:

a. those set by large firms in a concentrated industry.

b. always higher than nonadministered prices.

c. high because these firms set target sales levels.

d. often the result of sales wars.

e. caused by labor unions.

15. External costs in the form of environmental damage are not handled well by free markets because:

a. the firm can produce their product without paying for damage to the environment.

b. the benefits of the clean-up accrue to only people outside the firm.

c. regulations require that the firm "internalize" these costs.

d. they would be inflationary.

e. they are caused by monopolies.

16. Regulation will tend to be inflationary if:

a. it is expensive for firms to abide by the regulations.

b. they restrict competition.

c. the regulation is costly to administer.

d. the regulations prevent firms from operating efficiently.

e. all of the above.

17. From 1958 to 1980, U.S. real per capita income:

a. almost doubled.

b. increased 4.5 times.

c. tripled.

d. remained stable.

e. fell due to the severe inflation in the late 1970s.

18. Indexation:

a. guarantees that certain incomes will not be hurt by inflation.

b. would maintain constant real incomes.

c. would keep interest rates low.

d. would adjust tax rates so that the government would not receive higher tax revenues.

e. none of the above.

19. Improved productivity will reduce inflation pressures by:

a. reducing aggregate demand.

b. increasing the incomes of workers.

c. increasing the supply of goods and services.

d. improving the rate of return on capital.

e. reducing the need for increases in the money supply.

20. President Nixon's program of wage–price controls in the early 1970s appeared successful largely because:

   a. there was excess capacity and thus, little inflationary pressure in the economy when they were started.

   b. the Council on Wage and Price Stability effectively monitored all wage and price changes.

   c. the controlled prices were able to act as signals for an efficient allocation of resources.

   d. prices were not allowed to increase *or* decrease.

   e. there were a large number of price changes in anticipation of the controls.

ANSWERS

Reviewing the Chapter

1. inflation
2. prices
3. unless they anticipated the different inflation rates, they underestimated your college expenses
4. increase
5. encourage production by maintaining positive profits in most industries
6. taxation, bonds, money
7. on
8. should not
9. fall
10. cost-push
11. over time, the contribution to the total product from one type of resource may increase or decrease
12. increased capital per unit of labor, increased skills of workers
13. stagflation
14. fully employed
15. concentrated, more
16. rubber, metals, automotive equipment, machinery
17. the number or sizes of these firms, the types of material inputs used in production, the types of labor required by modern technology, and the skills of the available labor pool
18. 70
19. 10
20. income tax rates increase with nominal increases in income, thus generating ever larger tax revenues even when real incomes may not have risen

Self-Evaluation Exercises and Applications

1. Many economists feel that a program of wage–price guidelines cannot be successful unless the guidelines are consistent with the underlying inflation trends in the economy. If the government's monetary and fiscal policies push the economy to try and expand at a more rapid rate than the guidelines, the guidelines cannot work. If the aggregate demand and supply situation supports a slower rate of inflation than

the guidelines suggest, the guidelines are unnecessary but will "work." Other problems posed by the guidelines are the interference in resource allocation they impose on the market and their administrative costs.

2. Inflation policies:
   a. Cost-push inflation can be controlled through decreasing aggregate demand, but would also be helped by reducing the power of labor unions and by increasing productivity.
   b. Demand-pull inflation can be controlled through decreasing aggregate demand.
   c. Stagflation can be helped by increasing productivity and perhaps by tax cuts that encourage more incentives to increase output.
   d. Inflation caused by monopoly's power to raise prices can be controlled by decreasing the power of the monopolies.
   e. Inflation accompanying high unemployment is the most difficult form of inflation—the solutions are not apparent and may include some of the same prescriptions used for stagflation.

3. Price controls:
   Price controls encourage excess demand and shortages since at control price P_1, suppliers will be willing to sell only quantity Q_2—for which quantity, consumers would be willing to pay as much as P_2. For this reason, it would be difficult to maintain controls for long.

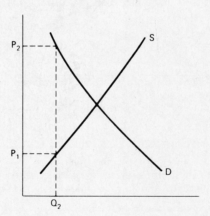

Chapter Test
True/False Questions
1. true	4. false	7. true	10. false
2. true	5. true	8. false	
3. true	6. true	9. true	

Multiple-Choice Questions
1. c; 2. a; 3. e; 4. a; 5. e; 6. e; 7. c; 8. b; 9. e; 10. a; 11. e; 12. b; 13. e; 14. a; 15. a; 16. e; 17. a; 18. a; 19. c; 20. a.

CHAPTER 11
Unemployment

CAPSULE SUMMARY

Unemployment is defined very carefully in this chapter. The likelihood of being unemployed, the government's policies of assisting the unemployed, the causes of unemployment, the relation between unemployment and inflation, the impact of minimum wages on unemployment, the types of unemployment, and the long-term prospects for unemployment are all studied.

The chapter asks whether some of our government policies might not actually increase unemployment, rather than reduce it or offset its negative effects, as intended. If strict government regulations and generous unemployment benefits reduce the incentives for firms to hire labor, and for labor to accept jobs, these policies may be creating worse employment conditions than would exist in their absence.

REVIEWING THE CHAPTER

1. The classical theory that perfect markets would always ensure full employment hasn't

   worked recently because wages are not flexible in a/an _____

   (downward, upward) direction, business _____ and the market

   power of labor _____ have destroyed the assumption of perfectly

   competitive markets, and structural changes have taken place in the labor market.

   (214)

2. The GNP gap measures the quantity of goods and services that could have been pro-

   duced by a full-employment economy in comparison with the _____

   production. (214)

3. The GNP gap _____ (can, cannot) be negative. (214–215)

4. The unemployment rate is the percentage of the _____

   who are out of work *and* presently looking for a job. (215)

5. A discouraged worker (one who has stopped looking for a job) _____

   (is, is not) counted as a part of the labor force. (215)

6. The Employment Act of 1946 clearly assigns the responsibility for maintaining full employment with the _____. (215)

7. Three primary forms of unemployment are _____, _____, and _____. (215–216)

8. The present unemployment rate in the U.S. is _____%, and this compares _____ (favorably, unfavorably) with the rate of _____% in your state.

9. If industrial expansion proceeded at exactly the same rate as the growth of resources and productivity, there would be little cause for _____ unemployment. (216)

10. Cyclical unemployment tends to be higher in the _____ (durable, nondurable) goods industries because the purchase of those goods can be _____ until income levels are improved. (216)

11. Regular unemployment benefits typically last for the first _____ (two, six, twelve) months a person is unemployed. Benefits average _____ (one quarter, one half, full) salary earned before being unemployed. (217)

12. Supplemental unemployment benefits are typically financed by the _____ (government, workers, employers). (217)

13. Public service employment _____ (may, may not) be inflationary if those newly created jobs compete with employment opportunities in the private sector. This would be most likely to happen when the overall unemployment rate was _____ (low, high). (217)

14. High rates of inflation tend to be more prevalent when unemployment is _____. The relation between these two variables is shown on a _____ curve. (217–218)

15. The unemployment rate for 1980 averaged 7% and the inflation rate averaged 12%.

Plot this as a new point on Figure 11.2. This point is _____ (below, on, above) the historical Phillips curve. (218)

16. The number of additional workers unemployed because of the increase in the minimum wage from $3.15 to $3.35 is _____ if D_1 is the relevant demand curve. A more elastic demand curve, D_2, would generate _____ (less, the same, more) unemployment. The demand curve for unskilled workers tends to be _____ (less, more) elastic than that for skilled workers. (222)

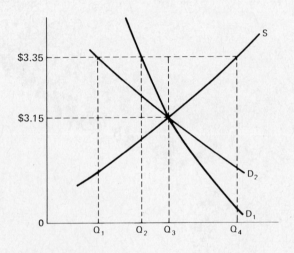

17. Minimum-wage laws will always be beneficial to poor people if the quantity _____ of poor workers does not decrease. (222)

18. Greater experience, skills, education, and training all tend to _____ (decrease, increase) the likelihood of unemployment. (222–223)

19. New government regulations and projections of high inflation rates might discourage businesses from expanding output because both of these will increase production _____ (costs, incomes, profits). (224–225)

20. When the government runs deficits, and borrows money to finance those deficits, the demand for funds to borrow _____ (decreases, increases) and the costs of borrowing those funds will _____ (decrease, increase). (225)

SELF-EVALUATION EXERCISES AND APPLICATIONS

1. There is evidence that the Phillips curve has shifted to the right. Describe that evidence and explain the possible implications for the economy.

2. The minimum wage increased on January 1, 1979, from $2.65 to $2.90 per hour, which was a 9.4% increase. President Carter had imposed a program of wage guidelines that limited wage increases to 7% (although wages under $4 per hour were to be exempt). Carter recommended that Congress enact a "real wage insurance" package, which would guarantee that workers could receive higher wages if inflation exceeded the 7% guideline. Minimum-wage earners were not to be eligible for the real wage insurance program since they received a 9.4% increase. Yet these are the lowest paid workers in the economy, and they may suffer the most from inflation. Should they have been eligible? Why or why not?

3. The Humphrey-Hawkins Act of 1978 promised to cut the unemployment rate to 4% in five years. Was this a realistic goal? What policy instruments should have been used toward this goal? What inflationary repercussions might have resulted?

CHAPTER TEST

True/False Questions

T   F   1. In a perfectly competitive system, money wages would fall if there were unemployment, but real wages would be unchanged since prices would also adjust downward.

T   F   2. If there is a GNP gap in one year, the production during the next year can compensate for the loss in the previous year.

T   F   3. Employment and unemployment can both be increasing at the same time.

T   F   4. The purchasing power of unemployment benefits exceeds the apparent monetary value because they are untaxed.

T   F   5. The comprehensive Employment and Training Act of 1974 provides federal funding for local jobs in areas where the unemployment rate exceeds 6½%.

T   F   6. The groups of people most likely to receive higher wages when there is an increase in the minimum wage are the lowest skilled workers, *if* they continue to be employed.

T   F   7. The minimum wage would have no effect on employment if it were set at the equilibrium wage rate.

T   F   8. Unemployment rates for whites have averaged approximately one half of the comparable rates for blacks.

T   F   9. The available capital per worker has decreased in the past 20 years in the U.S.

T   F   10. Reducing the length of the work week to four days would go a long way toward solving the problems of cyclical unemployment.

Multiple-Choice Questions

1. In a perfect market system, unemployment can't be a problem because:
    a. if the demand for workers decreased, their price would increase.
    b. prices for labor are flexible in an upward direction but do not decrease easily.
    c. employers would hire more of the unemployed workers at the prevailing wages.
    d. if price of labor fell, quantity demanded would increase.
    e. the derived demand curve for labor would shift to the right.

2. The GNP gap:
    a. can never be recovered.
    b. results in unemployment.
    c. lowers real incomes.
    d. is the difference between actual and potential output.
    e. all of the above.

3. The labor force does not include:
    a. those presently employed full time.
    b. those who haven't looked for a job in the past two months.
    c. those who work in a family business without being paid.
    d. part-time workers.
    e. second workers in a family.

4. Some unemployment serves a useful function in the economy. This is because:
   a. it reflects the transition of workers between jobs.
   b. it usually includes a greater percentage of women and teenagers.
   c. it reflects recovery from a cyclical downturn.
   d. there is imperfect correlation between the skills of the workers and the needs of industry.
   e. it is concentrated in the durable goods industries, which are less necessary to consumers than the nondurables, such as food.

5. The most effective policy to cure the structural unemployment apparent in our economy is:
   a. monetary policy.
   b. fiscal policy.
   c. countercyclical policy.
   d. increased unemployment benefits.
   e. skill-training programs.

6. Logical explanations for a rightward shift in the Phillips curve would *not* include:
   a. expectations of higher inflation.
   b. more government training programs to match skills with jobs.
   c. less incentives to work since the government guarantees some income without work.
   d. increased use of consumer credit.
   e. structural shifts in the economy.

7. The group in the labor force that experiences the highest rate of unemployment is:
   a. white men over 19.
   b. women over 19.
   c. black men over 19.
   d. white teenagers.
   e. black teenagers.

8. Capital investment in the U.S. may expand soon because:
   a. fiscal policies have been contractionary.
   b. corporate tax rates have fallen.
   c. unemployment has increased.
   d. interest costs have increased.
   e. none of the above.

9. Unemployment will typically increase when:
   a. there is a business recovery.
   b. wage rates decrease.
   c. government transfer payments decrease.
   d. the Phillips curve shifts to the left.
   e. the GNP gap increases.

10. Business cycles are less severe today than they were earlier in the twentieth century because:
    a. the government has better control over monetary and fiscal policies.
    b. interest rates are lower.
    c. capital expansion has slowed.
    d. consumers spend a greater proportion of their incomes on durable goods than they did earlier.
    e. minimum wages have provided an earnings floor for low-income workers.

11. Unemployment rates can decrease when:
    a. employment is falling.
    b. employment is rising.
    c. the labor force is growing.
    d. the labor force is shrinking.
    e. all of the above.

12. Frictional unemployment is necessary because:
    a. not all people who could be in the labor force are presently seeking jobs.
    b. dynamic labor markets include workers changing jobs.
    c. unions restrict entry to some jobs.
    d. more workers have two jobs to help maintain an adequate standard of living.
    e. many workers hold positions in the "underground" economy.

13. Employment in manufacturing durables is very cyclically sensitive because:
    a. durable purchases can be postponed.
    b. durables last a long time.
    c. employees making durables do not have job contracts that protect their positions.
    d. in bad economic times, consumers will spend a greater proportion of their incomes on nondurables.
    e. all of the above.

14. Programs such as unemployment benefits designed to assist those who have lost their jobs may also work to reduce employment since:
    a. workers have to be seeking employment to be eligible.
    b. unemployment benefits are very low.
    c. they come close to offsetting the wages lost from the job.
    d. some unemployed workers are able to obtain public service jobs.
    e. none of the above.

15. The Phillips curve appears to have shifted to the right as a result of:
    a. structural problems within the economy.
    b. expectations of high unemployment levels.
    c. a lower "natural rate" of unemployment.
    d. a reduction of public service job opportunities.
    e. poorly functioning financial markets.

16. Raising the level of minimum wages is likely to result in:
    a. less employment.
    b. increased inflation.
    c. increased costs to employers.
    d. pay raises to some workers not directly affected by the minimums.
    e. all of the above.

17. If the demand for all workers affected by the minimum wage was perfectly inelastic (i.e., the demand curve was parallel to the Y-axis), the unemployment caused by the minimum wage would be:
    a. zero.
    b. very little.
    c. a moderate amount.
    d. a greal deal.
    e. impossible to estimate.

18. Capital shortages could be reduced by:
    a. increased pollution and safety regulations on business.
    b. price and wage controls.
    c. training the labor force more carefully.
    d. increasing tax incentives for investment.
    e. inflationary government policies.

19. If there isn't another increase in the legal minimum wage, so that the 1981 minimum of $3.35 prevails into the mid-1980s,
    a. the real value of the minimum wage will increase.
    b. the non-minimum-wage workers will be at a competitive disadvantage.
    c. the impact of the nominal wage will be reduced as inflation raises average workers' salaries.
    d. employment in minimum-wage jobs will be reduced.
    e. labor markets will be further from equilibrium levels of employment than they now are.

20. Four-day workweeks might:
    a. reduce unemployment.
    b. reduce employee transportation costs.
    c. increase productivity.
    d. increase available vacation time.
    e. all are possible outcomes.

ANSWERS

Reviewing the Chapter
1. downward, monopolies, unions
2. actual
3. cannot
4. labor force
5. is not
6. government
7. frictional, cyclical, structural
8. (Check with a local newspaper or government agency for the current national figure and your state unemployment figure.)
9. cyclical
10. durables, postponed
11. six, one half
12. employers
13. may, low
14. low, Phillips
15. above
16. $Q_3 - Q_2$, more, more
17. demanded
18. decrease
19. costs
20. increases, increase

Self-Evaluation Exercises and Applications

1. The Phillips curve has moved to the right because levels of unemployment accompanying each inflation rate are higher than they were in the 1960s and early 1970s. The implication for economic policy is that it has become more difficult to achieve the relatively low rate of unemployment of that earlier period. Changes in the composition of the labor force and the disincentives have probably caused this shift.

2. The answer to this question is largely a matter of opinion. The situation posed by the question points to another policy dilemma presented by the wage–price guidelines.

3. A 4% unemployment rate may not be achievable without considerably increasing inflation pressures. Since a larger proportion of the labor force represents second workers in a family, and since the government underwrites income decreases through unemployment payments and welfare benefits, a given level of unemployment has less adverse impact on families than it once did. The best instruments for lowering unemployment rates are job-training programs and reducing taxes.

Chapter Test

True/False Questions

1. true
2. false
3. true
4. true
5. true
6. true
7. true
8. true
9. false
10. false

Multiple-Choice Questions

1. d; 2. e; 3. b; 4. a; 5. e; 6. b; 7. e; 8. b; 9. e; 10. a; 11. e; 12. b; 13. e;
14. c; 15. a; 16. e; 17. a; 18. d; 19. c; 20. e.

CHAPTER 12

Poverty and Income Distribution

CAPSULE SUMMARY

The solution to poverty depends very much on the causes of those low incomes. Categorical poverty, insular poverty, and poverty caused by cyclical downturns in the economy all have different causes and, therefore, very different cures.

The U.S. system for income redistribution has reduced income differentials over time. However, very little progress has been made recently. Much of the U.S. redistribution is in the form of categorical grants or transfers of services. An alternative system, that of a negative income tax system, is examined.

Social Security is a system of funding programs for retired people. The sources of income for Social Security are the payroll taxes that current workers pay. These have increased rapidly in the past ten years and are scheduled to increase even further. Alternatives to Social Security are discussed.

REVIEWING THE CHAPTER

1. The official definition of poverty used in the U.S. multiplies the cost of an adequate diet by _____ (two, three, four, five) and adjusts for varying circumstances of the family. (230)

2. Approximately _____% (12, 20, 25) of American families have less income than the poverty line. Almost _____ (one third, one half) of the poor families are those headed by a female. (230)

3. _____ (Insular, Business cycle, Categorical) poverty is best treated by using expansionary monetary and fiscal policies. (231)

4. Equality of economic opportunity often yields very _____ (equal, unequal) distribution of the economic pie. (233)

5. Benefits payments under Social Security are payable primarily based on _____ (need, past contribution). (241)

6. The largest portion of the OASDHI income transfer program is _____ benefits, primarily Social Security benefits to retirees. (233)

7. _____ results when two people are treated differently on some basis other than individual merit. (236)

8. An employer, in deciding to hire worker A rather than worker B, may not be actively discriminating since the worker A may have more training than worker B. However, the reason that worker A has had more training may be due to past _____. (233)

9. If government reduces the benefits of an aid program dollar-for-dollar as earned income grows, the effective tax rate is _____%. (235)

10. A negative income tax is a form of a _____ grant from the government to families. (234)

11. If a negative income tax guaranteed $3000 per family, the tax rate were 50%, and a family earned $1000, the net payment to that family would be $_____. (234)

12. Disincentive effects of negative income taxes can be reduced by _____ _____. (234)

13. If direct grants increase incomes, and the economy is close to full employment, they may also cause increased _____. (234)

14. Economic analysis differs from _____ analysis primarily because in economic analysis it is very difficult to hold all the variables constant except the one being tested. (238–239)

15. If the goal of a federal program were to raise as many people as possible above the poverty line with a given number of dollars, the program would be _____ (least, most) successful if those dollars were distributed to the families just below the poverty line, rather than to the poorest families. (239)

16. There has been considerable reduction in _____ (absolute, relative) poverty but little change in _____ (absolute, relative) poverty in our country in the past ten years. (240)

17. A _____ curve illustrates relative shares of income. If all income were evenly distributed, the curve would be _____. (240)

18. If government transfer programs (such as food stamps) were included as income, the current income distribution would be _____ (less, more) equal than it appears today. (243)

19. List several reasons for the increase in the number of urban poor. (243–244)

    a. _____

    _____

    b. _____

    _____

20. Many federal programs are funded at state level, which probably _____ (increases, decreases) the availability of federal aid to urban areas. (244)

SELF-EVALUATION EXERCISES AND APPLICATIONS

1. In the past twenty years, the number of families under the poverty line has decreased by 50%. What are the possibilities for diminishing the poverty population by another 50% by year 2000? Support your answer.

2. The median income of women is only slightly greater than half of that of men in the same occupation. However, when education and skill levels, length of employment in that job, and full-time job status are equal, that difference is reduced to 15%. Which is the more appropriate measure of discrimination and why?

3. Can you describe circumstances in which two families each had $6000 of income and yet one was "poor" and the other not? List some of these circumstances. Do you feel that a more relevant definition of poverty might include the average of lifetime earnings, rather than one year's earnings? Why or why not? Would the lifetime definition be a useful operational tool for the government in establishing redistribution policies? Why or why not?

4. Draw a typical Lorenz Curve and show how a decrease in the top personal income-tax rates would shift the curve.

CHAPTER TEST

True/False Questions

T   F   1. Families are more likely to be poor if they live in urban rather than rural surroundings.

T   F   2. Almost all poor families do not have a member who is actively employed.

T   F   3. Insular poverty results from structural unemployment and is usually concentrated geographically.

T   F   4. The economic harm from discrimination extends beyond the lower incomes earned by the groups actually suffering from the discrimination.

T   F   5. Personal income-tax exemptions only benefit those taxpayers whose tax liability exceeds the value of the exemption.

T   F   6. Aid to Families with Dependent Children is a program that has resulted in tremendous increases in the labor-force participation of the mothers in the program.

T   F   7. If a government program results in moving the Lorenz Curve closer to the diagonal line, it has succeeded in reducing income poverty.

T   F   8. If the ratio of income earners to retirees under Social Security is expected to fall by 50% in the next fifty years, the cost to each worker of maintaining the existing benefit package will have to increase by 50%.

T   F   9. A regressive tax is one that takes a higher percentage of income from the rich than from the poor.
T   F   10. If the Social Security system reduced its benefit plan to insure fiscal solvency, more retired people would probably fall beneath the poverty line.

Multiple-Choice Questions

1. The subgroup of the population that is most likely to be poor is:
   a. white families headed by a female.
   b. black families headed by a female.
   c. white families headed by a male.
   d. black families headed by a male.
   e. both b and d.

2. Categorical poverty:
   a. could be alleviated by moving factories to those areas where the poor are concentrated.
   b. would be helped if the poor were moved to cities.
   c. could be alleviated through expansionary monetary and fiscal policy.
   d. requires regular governmental income transfers.
   e. none of the above.

3. The aid programs that have been used to alleviate categorical poverty are *not* criticized because they:
   a. are very expensive.
   b. may discourage work effort.
   c. encourage fathers to desert their families.
   d. are not available to all of the poor.
   e. help people who have few alternative sources of income.

4. Direct grant programs:
   a. would necessarily be more expensive than our present poverty programs.
   b. would be more complex to administer than our present poverty programs.
   c. would allow consumers to choose how they wanted to spend their incomes.
   d. are used primarily in underdeveloped countries.
   e. would require the recipient to qualify as a member of an eligible category.

5. It would be possible to reduce poverty by:
   a. reducing race and sex discrimination.
   b. large-scale income transfers from the rich to the poor.
   c. improving work incentives.
   d. changing the definition of poverty.
   e. all of the above.

6. If relative income shares are to be more equal:
   a. a more progressive income tax could be passed.
   b. monetary and fiscal policies could be more expansionary.
   c. labor unions would have to decline in importance.
   d. more people should receive elementary education.
   e. all of the above.

7. The present problems of the Social Security system are *not* a result of:
   a. demographic changes.
   d. increased inflation.
   b. higher tax rates on workers.
   e. earlier retirement.
   c. increased benefits.
8. Some programs of the federal government that have worsened the problems of the cities include:
   a. building highway arteries into the city.
   b. mass-transportation projects.
   c. public employment grants.
   d. income transfer programs.
   e. rental subsidies for low-income housing.
9. The negative income-tax experiments with work incentives have found that incomes tend to increase slightly but the number of hours worked tends to decrease slightly. This result can be explained by:
   a. longer time spent finding a job.
   b. higher wage rates.
   c. less labor-force participation of marginally productive workers.
   d. less "moonlighting" (holding down two jobs) and thus higher productivity on the main job.
   e. all of the above.
10. The Social Security program includes:
    a. negative income taxes.
    d. housing subsidies.
    b. Medicare and Medicaid programs.
    e. food stamps.
    c. private pension plans.
11. The official government definition of poverty was derived from:
    a. the level of transfers available to a family.
    b. minimum housing requirements.
    c. an average level of U.S. income.
    d. minimum nutritional standards.
    e. an analysis of all the needs of the poor.
12. Cyclical poverty can be offset by:
    a. reducing the severity of business fluctuations.
    b. income transfers.
    c. monetary policies designed to promote economic stability.
    d. fiscal policies that increase aggregate demand during business downturns.
    e. all of the above.
13. Policies that followed the philosophy of Social Darwinism would avow:
    a. large income transfers to the poor.
    b. heavy tax rates on the rich.
    c. negative income taxes.
    d. widespread incentives for production.
    e. equality of incomes.
14. Insular poverty has been alleviated by programs that:
    a. retain workers.
    b. move workers to regions where there are low unemployment rates.
    c. relocate businesses to the poverty areas.

d. improve placement services for unemployed workers.

e. all of the above.

15. Social Security payments:

a. are designed to prevent business cycle poverty.

b. provide benefits based on past contributions for the majority of their recipients.

c. are included in the food stamp program.

d. are funded by federal corporate income taxes.

e. are mostly based on financial need.

16. The primary reason that the major antipoverty program in the U.S. is *not* one of direct income transfers is that:

a. it would be too costly.

b. income transfers couldn't be designed to maintain work incentives.

c. income transfers are too difficult to administer.

d. if direct grants were added to the other programs, they might be inflationary.

e. the poor can't be trusted to properly spend the income.

17. Discrimination against females is likely to result in:

a. lower wages for women.

b. loss of output for the economy as a whole.

c. an inefficient allocation of resources.

d. an underrepresentation of females in executive positions.

e. all of the above.

18. The 1980 poverty level for an urban family of four was approximately:

a. $2000.   d. $8000.

b. $4000.   e. $10,000.

c. $6000.

19. Lorenz Curves depicting relative income shares in the U.S. show that:

a. wealth is unevenly distributed throughout the population of the U.S.

b. relative income shares have not changed over the past twenty years.

c. a progressive income tax has reduced the share available to the rich in the past ten years.

d. the poorest 20% of the people receive only 10% of the income.

e. the richest 20% of the people receive 30% of the income.

20. Some of the long-term financial troubles of the Social Security program could be solved by:

a. emergency grants.

b. raising the retirement age of workers.

c. increasing the benefits to the elderly.

d. adding other programs to the Social Security system.

e. reducing taxes on current workers.

ANSWERS

Reviewing the Chapter

1. three
2. twelve, one half

3. business cycle
4. unequal
5. past contributions
6. insured
7. discrimination
8. discrimination
9. 100
10. direct
11. 2500
12. very low tax rates on the earned portion of the income
13. inflation
14. scientific
15. most
16. absolute, relative
17. Lorenz, a straight diagonal line across the square
18. more
19. a. marginal agricultural workers leaving farms and looking for work in the cities
    b. use of assembly-line methods of manufacture that are land intensive, thus moving factories to the suburbs
    c. loss of tax base of cities
    d. increased need for welfare and other services in cities
20. decreases

Self-Evaluation Exercises and Applications

1. Poverty can be easily reduced another 50% by redefining the poverty line or by holding the official definition constant when inflation progresses. The poverty population can be reduced through education and training programs and by income transfer programs through the federal government.

2. The results of income comparisons between men and women vary with the researcher. However, all research seems to indicate a significant difference in earnings when "all other things are equal." This is probably due to discrimination and should be corrected before income equity between the sexes is achieved.

3. Absolute income differences do not reflect differences in family size, age of the family, needs of the family, location, and responsibilities. They also ignore the crucial question as to whether there are alternatives available to the family to its current income level (e.g., a poor writer who could also be a reporter for a newspaper, a college student who could have a job). Lifetime earnings do give a much better picture of poverty but would be difficult to use for governmental redistribution policies since information on lifetime earnings wouldn't be available until the end of the lifetime.

4. Lorenz Curve: Shift from _____ to _____.

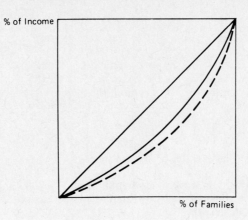

% of Income

% of Families

Chapter Test

True/False Questions

1. false	4. true	7. true	10. true
2. false	5. true	8. true	
3. true	6. false	9. false	

Multiple-Choice Questions

1. b; 2. d; 3. e; 4. c; 5. e; 6. a; 7. b; 8. a; 9. e; 10. b; 11. d; 12. e; 13. d;
14. e; 15. b; 16. d; 17. e; 18. d; 19. b; 20. b.

CHAPTER 13

Economic Growth

CAPSULE SUMMARY

Previous chapters have defined GNP, measured GNP, and modeled GNP; this chapter asks whether a large GNP is desirable and how different countries can have such divergent capacities to produce.

Two growth theories are reviewed. The *sectoral theory* says that there is a systematic growth pattern that all economies follow—first agriculture develops, then the manufacturing sector, then the service industries. The *export-base theory* suggests that economic development cannot occur without a strong industry producing exportable commodities.

Negative externalities are one of the less desirable features of growth. Ways to control these externalities and force the users of the products whose manufacture has created the negative impacts are examined.

REVIEWING THE CHAPTER

1. Increasing gross national product _____ (does, does not) necessarily increase welfare. (248)

2. If the population is expanding and growth of GNP is zero or negative, the per capita income must be _____ (falling, constant, rising). (248)

3. The growth of potential GNP is limited by the quantity and quality of _____ available, the level of _____ knowledge, and the system of organizing the resources. (249)

4. Population increases tend to be associated with increased growth since the resource of _____ has expanded and the higher incomes increase the _____ for the goods produced. (249)

5. If consumption equals income, savings must be _____. Investment is only possible when there is _____ savings. (249–250)

6. Walter Rostow used an analogy between a country's growth patterns and an airplane's takeoff. He argued that there were several conditions that were necessary before the country could grow, just as an airplane had to be moving sufficiently

rapidly before it could take off. These preconditions include _____

_____

_____. (250)

7. Economic growth is difficult to maintain in a _____ (developing, mature) economy because the need for new products and services diminishes. (251)

8. When a mature economy needs additional growth in demand, the government can encourage production of additional _____ goods, such as schools, swimming pools, and tennis courts. (251)

9. One possible automatic regulating device for an economic system is population. Malthus agreed that when resources were plentiful, population would _____ (decrease, increase), and this trend would continue until the population was barely at subsistence levels of consumption. (251)

10. Two factors that potentially can limit growth are inadequate supplies of _____ and excessive _____. (251)

11. An environmental _____ describes the limited quantity of resources available. An environmental _____ describes the minimum quantity of fresh air and clean water necessary for life. (252)

12. Linear growth involves increments of the same magnitude in each time period, whereas _____ growth involves increments of greater magnitude in each successive time period. (252)

13. If the correct theory of growth is one that emphasizes stages of growth by sector, the first sector to grow is typically _____, followed by _____, and finally the _____ sector. (253)

14. Export-based growth assumes that a country has a resource or commodity that another country wants to _____, which generates _____ in the exporting country, which aids economic development. (253)

15. A rich country is able to increase its capital stock more rapidly than a poor country because it _____

_____

_____

This will result in a _____ (greater, same, lesser) shift outward of the future production possibility curve of the rich country than/as that of the poor country. (257)

16. Side effects of the production process are called _____. (257)

17. When there are social costs and benefits, the market process may not operate efficiently to balance total benefits with total _____. This is often used as an argument to have some _____ interaction in those markets. (258)

18. In deciding who will be given the limited resources available for world aid, governments may use the principle of triage, giving aid to those who _____

_____. (260)

19. An input–output model of the economy is helpful in identifying scarce _____ and defining bottlenecks in the process of _____. (261)

20. Per capita income in developed countries exceeds by _____ times that of underdeveloped countries. (261–262)

SELF-EVALUATION EXERCISES AND APPLICATIONS

1. Much of the evidence from developed countries points to the fact that the key factor for future growth is current savings. How does an underdeveloped country, which barely produces enough output for subsistence, increase its savings? Should the government play a role? What about international aid?

2. The 1970s saw major changes in regional growth patterns in the U.S., primarily away from the snowbelt and toward the sunbelt. Can we assume that growth rates within the various regions in the U.S. will automatically equalize? Why or why not?

3. Below is a sample matrix describing the input–output relationship between five products and five resources. Define hypothetical inputs and outputs by placing numbers in the spaces that are empty.

| | Consuming Sectors | | | | | |
	Metals	Machines	Fuel	Agriculture	Labor	Output
Producing Sectors						
Metals	25	30	15	10	20	100
Machines						
Fuel						
Agriculture						
Labor						

What happens when the labor supply is increased? How would each sector be affected?

CHAPTER TEST

True/False Questions

T   F   1. Per capita growth has averaged 4% per year for the past fifty years.

T   F   2. The question of whether or not to limit growth is an important one for rich nations but is largely irrelevant for underdeveloped and poor countries.

T   F   3. An export-based theory of growth would suggest that increased development would not be possible through investment in an agricultural commodity.

T   F   4. Frequently, different theories of economic development lead to very different policy prescriptions.

T   F   5. Externalities of production are negative; thus, production levels should be lower.

T   F   6. When there are significant externalities, the market cannot operate efficiently because the benefits and costs extend beyond those who pay for the product.

T   F   7. Equity and efficiency are often equated where there aren't any externalities.

T   F   8. Petroleum prices and supplies are very important in the production of fertilizer.

T   F   9. It is impossible for an economy to be simultaneously faced with unlimited wants and unemployed resources.

T   F   10. The only way to obtain zero economic growth would be to have zero population growth.

Multiple-Choice Questions

1. Which of the following will cause GNP to decrease?
   a. an increase in population.
   b. an increase in homegrown vegetables rather than purchased vegetables.
   c. inflation.
   d. an increase in the labor-force participation of women.
   e. increases in pollution.

2. If a country is at a subsistence level of income:
   a. savings will be zero.
   b. all income is consumed.
   c. investment will be zero.
   d. it will be difficult to raise per capita income.
   e. all of the above.

3. The primary problem faced by a mature economy is:
   a. finding a way to maintain full employment.
   b. maintaining quality products.
   c. preventing population explosions.
   d. wasteful advertising.
   e. preventing pollution.

4. If the arguments in the Club of Rome's *Limits to Growth* are correct, our economy must:
   a. increase production to feed our growing population.
   b. search diligently for new supplies of energy to support increased production.
   c. restrict the growth of output to protect our environment.
   d. prevent linear changes in environmental quality.
   e. lower the ceilings limiting available resources.

5. In a sectoral-growth theory the manufacturing sector can grow:
   a. only after agricultural productivity has increased faster than the need for agricultural products, releasing labor for manufacturing.
   b. as transportation develops to connect small communities into larger markets.
   c. before the growth of the service sector.
   d. before the limits to growth have been reached.
   e. all of the above.
6. One of the following is *not* an example of a negative externality:
   a. noise pollution.
   b. junked cars.
   c. increases in resources used in production.
   d. water pollution.
   e. social costs.
7. The Green Revolution:
   a. will end when fertilizer supplies become scarce.
   b. occurred in the first half of the twentieth century.
   c. resulted in large increases in farm productivity in Asian countries.
   d. was largely a result of increasing the quantity of land used in agriculture.
   e. reduced the world's stockpiles of food reserves.
8. Increasing worldwide agricultural production would *not* be possible by:
   a. increasing the quantity of land used.
   b. reducing the grain input to meat production in the U.S.
   c. increasing the use of fertilizer.
   d. using more irrigation on the available land.
   e. reducing the world's population.
9. An input–output model can be expected to:
   a. identify shortages in resources.
   b. define quantities of pollution.
   c. compare consumption and savings levels.
   d. describe the effects of new technology.
   e. all of the above.
10. Most development theories assume that after an initial thrust of growth, development will automatically spread to the rest of the economy. This does not always happen because:
    a. prices will increase due to inflation.
    b. the initial thrust may be too great for the economy to handle.
    c. incomes earned in the favored sector may not be spent in the less developed sector.
    d. the development problems of all countries are different.
    e. none of the above.
11. Historically, the rate of growth of GNP has averaged:
    a. 2%.
    b. 4%.
    c. 6%.
    d. 8%.
    e. 10%.

12. The production possibilities curve defines the:
    a. maximum quantity of output for a given time period.
    b. the opportunities costs of one type of output in comparison with another type of output.
    c. potential GNP.
    d. the limits to production as imposed by the quantity and quality of resources available.
    e. all of the above.
13. Mature economies face difficulty when they try to:
    a. provide the necessary intrastructure for development (e.g., roads, airports, harbors).
    b. maintain full employment.
    c. develop consumer goods industries.
    d. establish basic health and education standards.
    e. produce leisure goods.
14. Exponential growth implies that:
    a. there will be an increasing rate of growth.
    b. there will be a constant rate of growth.
    c. there will be a decreasing rate of growth.
    d. environmental ceilings and floors exist.
    e. the growth is the same amount in every time period.
15. Sectoral growth theories argue that:
    a. the agricultural sector will typically develop before the service sector.
    b. the transportation sector development will allow specialization and division of labor.
    c. the manufacturing sector will develop before the service sector.
    d. the history of past development efforts will repeat itself.
    e. all of the above.
16. The export-base theory of growth suggests that:
    a. growing countries must have large exports and imports.
    b. growth is dependent on an exportable commodity that generates income for domestic investment.
    c. agricultural production must increase beyond the needs of the country in question; then the farm products can be exported.
    d. growth must be carefully managed.
    e. the U.S. followed an export-based growth pattern.
17. Poor nations are likely to:
    a. have a production possibilities frontier that exceeds those of rich countries.
    b. have more negative externalities than rich nations.
    c. have smaller rates of population growth than rich nations.
    d. save less than rich countries.
    e. be able to define their production priorities more accurately than rich nations.
18. It is generally considered inequitable that:
    a. total benefits to society will equal total costs.
    b. some firms produce products that involve higher per unit costs than others.
    c. some firms earn higher profits than others.

d. firms can force society to pay for some of their negative externalities.

e. scarce resources must be allocated to satisfy unlimited wants.

19. The large increase anticipated in future crop production may be limited by the:

a. unavailability of petroleum as a base for fertilizer.

b. encroachment of residential and commercial development into farm land.

c. crop disasters.

d. decrease in water supplies available for irrigation.

e. all of the above.

20. Input-output studies show:

a. that planning for economic development is practically impossible.

b. that bottlenecks will always appear and prevent as high a growth rate as otherwise would be possible.

c. the cost of using various inputs.

d. how resources are allocated between different sectors in the economy.

e. that underdeveloped countries will soon catch up to developed countries in per capita output.

ANSWERS

Reviewing the Chapter

1. does not
2. falling
3. resources, technical
4. labor, demand
5. zero, positive
6. minimum levels of health, education, and motivation
7. mature
8. social
9. increase
10. resources, pollution
11. ceiling, floor
12. exponential
13. agricultural, manufacturing, service
14. import, income
15. has a greater proportion of its output above the subsistence level, greater
16. externalities
17. costs, community (government)
18. will survive with some aid instead of those who will survive with no aid or those who need a great deal of aid
19. supplies, growth
20. twelve

Self-Evaluation Exercises and Applications

1. An underdeveloped country can probably only increase its capital formation through forced savings (i.e., taxation) or through infusions of aid from external sources.

2. Growth rates between the various regions of the country should eventually be equalized if we assume that the market system works, and there seems to be good evidence

that it does in this case. Some of the advantages of the sunbelt states are reduced in the process of development. As firms locate where labor costs are low, they increase the demand for labor, which increases its price, reducing the labor cost differential. Similarly, as firms who are heavy energy-consumers move where energy is abundant and relatively cheap, and as energy costs increase more rapidly than other costs, the industries that are not high energy-users will have slower increases in costs and thus greater developmental advantages.

3. Input–output table:
   Any combination of inputs and outputs is possible for this table, as long as the output total reflects the horizontal summation of production in each sector. When labor supply is increased, the proportion of labor to total resources will increase and probably fewer other resources will be used in combination with the greater quantity of labor.

Chapter Test

True/False Questions

1. true	4. true	7. true	10. false
2. true	5. false	8. true	
3. false	6. true	9. false	

Multiple-Choice Questions

1. b; 2. e; 3. a; 4. c; 5. e; 6. c; 7. a; 8. e; 9. e; 10. c; 11. b; 12. e; 13. b; 14. a; 15. e; 16. b; 17. d; 18. d; 19. e; 20. d.

CHAPTER 14

International Trade and Finance

CAPSULE SUMMARY

This chapter uses demand and supply curves to place the entire U.S. economic situation in world perspective. It describes currency flows and why market forces cause changes in the prices of the various currencies. It analyzes historic attempts to stabilize the prices of different currencies.

One method used in the past to stabilize currencies was a gold standard. Many economists today believe that the U.S. should return to a gold standard, which would allow international economic phenomena to regulate our supply of money and, hence, our inflation rate.

The benefits and costs of open trading with the rest of the world are studied. The conclusion reached is that the world's production possibilities frontier will always be extended if free trade is allowed.

REVIEWING THE CHAPTER

1. The process of specialization makes one country or region _____

    (more, less) dependent on other regions. (266)

2. Specialization of production is easier with a _____ (large, small)

    market for selling goods. (266)

3. _____ (Absolute, Comparative, Absolute and comparative) advan-

    tage is implied by the following table: (266–268)

	Number of Units Which Can Be Produced per Labor Day	
	Shoes	Skis
Iceland	7	14
Poland	12	9

4. In the above example, total production could be increased if Iceland spent all its time

    producing _____ (shoes, skis) and Poland spent all its time produc-

    ing _____ (shoes, skis). (267–269)

5. Again, in the table used for question 3, the opportunity cost of having Iceland produce one pair of shoes is equal to _____ pairs of skis. The opportunity cost of having Poland produce one pair of shoes is equal to _____ pairs of skis. (269)

6. Trade is always advantageous when there are _____ (absolute, comparative, absolute and comparative) advantages between two countries. (267–270)

7. A constant curve _____ (is the same as, differs from) a normal production possibility curve because it assumes that _____ _____. (269)

8. Using Table 14.5, the largest dollar value of any category in the balance of payments account is _____. (272)

9. The value of exports and imports in the U.S. has _____ (increased, decreased) significantly in the past fifteen years. (272)

10. The price of a currency in relation to the monetary units of other countries is called the _____. (274)

11. When currency values can fluctuate in response to changes in supply and demand, an excess supply of a currency will result in a decrease in the _____ of that currency. This is also called _____ (depreciation, devaluation). (274)

12. If the price of a dollar decreases, American exports will _____ (decrease, increase). This is because a given quantity of a foreign currency can buy _____ (more, fewer) American dollars. (274)

13. A possible conflict exists between domestic monetary policy and a country's desire for stable capital flows. If a country is pursuing easy money, it will follow policies to _____ (raise, lower) interest rates. However, this change in rates will _____ (discourage, encourage) investment in that country. (274)

14. A _____ is a tax on imported goods that tends to _____ (decrease, increase) the price of those goods and reduce the quantity demanded. (275)

15. If identical goods are produced in two countries, and Country A can produce the good more inexpensively, the demand for Country A's production will increase, the price for the good produced in Country A will _____ (decrease, increase), the demand for Country B's production will _____ (decrease, increase), and the price for the good produced in Country B will _____ (decrease, increase) until the prices for the same goods in both countries approach _____. (278–279)

16. When an imported commodity hurts the sales of a domestic industry, a perfectly functioning market would shift the resources used to produce that good domestically _____ _____. (274, 275, 279)

17. Today, U.S. dollars _____ (are, are not) redeemable in gold. (281)

18. When President Roosevelt devalued the dollar in 1934, he _____ (increased, reduced) the number of ounces of gold that each dollar would buy. (282)

19. If all currencies were allowed to freely float, and there weren't any restrictions on trade or capital flows, balance-of-payments deficits and surpluses would all approach _____. (283)

20. Multinational corporations will _____ (decrease, increase) the world's production possibilities by allowing firms to produce where costs are _____ (highest, lowest). (284)

SELF-EVALUATION EXERCISES AND APPLICATIONS

1. A quota on an imported good restricts the supply of that good. If the quota were set at quantity Q_1 in the graph below, the effective supply would follow the line 124 and the price would be P_1. Without the quota, the price and quantity would be _____.

   Using this diagram, explain why the domestic producer of a competitive product would like to see this quota established.

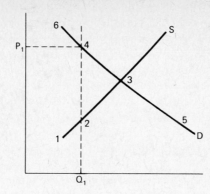

2. Throughout 1978, the value of the dollar continued to fall relative to the currencies of many of our trading partners. In November, President Carter announced a policy to stabilize the value of the dollar by contractionary monetary policy and by buying up large supplies of dollars that were held abroad. How was tighter money in the U.S. supposed to affect exports and imports, long-term capital investments, and international loans? How would the purchases of American dollars in Europe affect the price of the dollar? Did these policies achieve the goal of increasing the value of the dollar?

3. The oil-producing nations in the Mideast have complained that our inflation has forced them to increase the price of the oil that they sell to the U.S. Is this argument valid? Why or why not? Would your answer differ if these Mideastern countries never spent any of the dollars they earned from selling their oil in the U.S.? Why or why not?

CHAPTER TEST

True/False Questions

T   F   1. Specialization and trade will increase total production only when each country has an absolute advantage in the production of one good.

T   F   2. If all countries had exactly the same resources and skills, specialization and trade could not increase the total world production.

T   F   3. A nation with a net outflow on its balance of payments account has more unspent claims against the assets of other nations than those nations have against it.

T   F   4. If U.S. inflation is worse than that of our trading nations, our exports will probably increase, and our imports will fall.

T   F   5. When the forces of demand and supply set the currency value, that value is called a fixed exchange rate.

T   F   6. Depreciation of a currency involves a deliberate act of a government to lower the price of that currency.

T   F   7. Foreign investors own less than 1% of the total production assets of the U.S.

T   F   8. Retaliatory tariffs reduce the advantages of specialization and trade and lower the combined production possibility curve for the trading countries.

T   F   9. One disadvantage of a gold standard was that it subordinated domestic monetary policy to international events.

T   F   10. I have thoroughly enjoyed studying economics!

Multiple-Choice Questions

1. The following would *not* be a natural advantage of an economy encouraging specialization:
   a. an inexpensive source of power.
   b. sufficient rainfall for agricultural production.
   c. a rapidly growing money supply.
   d. specially trained labor.
   e. a deep harbor.

2. Balance of payments is a measure of:
   a. exports minus imports.
   b. imports minus exports.
   c. net capital inflows.
   d. comparative interest rates between two countries.
   e. all outflows minus all inflows.

3. Positive trade balances in the U.S. would be helped by:
   a. increased dependence on foreign oil.
   b. higher U.S. interest rates.
   c. an increase in the domestic income levels of other countries.
   d. greater military involvement in Europe.
   e. more U.S. citizens traveling in Asia.

4. If foreigners possess excess dollars, they may:
   a. buy more U.S. goods.

    b. travel in the U.S.

    c. invest in U.S. government bonds.

    d. buy U.S. real estate.

    e. all of the above.

5. An increase in the demand for Japanese yen would tend to:

    a. raise the price of the yen.   d. discourage exports out of Japan.

    b. encourage travel in Japan.   e. decrease investment in Japan.

    c. encourage imports into Japan.

6. Nontariff barriers to trade include the following:

    a. export subsidies.   d. tax exemptions for exports.

    b. import quotas.   e. all of the above.

    c. product standards for imports.

7. When the full gold standard was in existence:

    a. a low-priced country would lose gold.

    b. a high-priced country would accumulate gold.

    c. a high-priced country would develop a balance-of-payments surplus.

    d. gold flows into the low-priced country would increase its money supply.

    e. prices of the various currencies fluctuated widely.

8. The U.S. has exported inflation to other countries by:

    a. trying to maintain fixed exchange rates.

    b. allowing a large accumulation of American dollars abroad.

    c. heavy military spending abroad.

    d. increasing our domestic money supply at a faster rate than our productivity increased.

    e. all of the above.

9. Economists often support tariffs for "infant industries." These are justified to:

    a. permanently protect a new industry from foreign competition.

    b. raise the price of that industry's products relative to the foreign competition.

    c. protect high cost domestic industry.

    d. avoid dependence on foreign supplies of essential resources.

    e. none of the above.

10. Advantages of operating multinational enterprises include:

    a. lower prices for imported goods.

    b. lower taxes on profits brought back to the U.S.

    c. use of lower cost resources abroad.

    d. a means to reduce balance-of-payments deficits.

    e. a way to reduce the competitive edge of foreign business.

11. As the degree of specialization increases:

    a. interdependence also increases.

    b. division of labor becomes more typical.

    c. countries are able to exploit their comparative and absolute advantages to a greater extent.

    d. the world's production possibilities curve moves outward.

    e. all of the above.

12. Given the following production possibilities combinations of Jeffrey and Jeannette for producing bikes and skates, which of the following statements is *not* true?

	Number of Units That Can be Produced per Day of Labor:	
	Bikes	Skates
Jeffrey	5	6
Jeannette	3	6

    a. Jeffrey has a comparative advantage in the production of bikes.

    b. Jeffrey has an absolute advantage in the production of bikes.

    c. Jeannette should specialize in skate production, and Jeffrey, in bike production.

    d. the opportunity costs of producing skates for both Jeffrey and Jeannette are identical.

    e. specialization and trade can increase total output for Jeffrey and Jeannette.

13. The U.S. balance of payments will show a larger surplus if:

    a. imports increase.

    b. interest earnings on foreign investments fall.

    c. Europeans buy parts of our factories.

    d. U.S. citizens increasingly travel as tourists to Asia.

    e. Japanese cars absorb a larger portion of the U.S. domestic automobile demand.

14. The dollar will be likely to depreciate when:

    a. the value of the supply of dollars flowing out of the country exceeds the value of the other currencies coming in.

    b. a lower value is set on each ounce of gold.

    c. the U.S. exports more than it imports.

    d. the price of other currencies is falling rapidly.

    e. U.S. inflation rates are less than those of other countries.

15. A tariff on an import will shift the supply curve for that product because:

    a. the manufacturer will try to produce at lower costs to offset the tariff.

    b. fewer imports will be purchased when the price increases.

    c. the tax increase is exactly equal to the increase in the price that must be paid for the import.

    d. it acts like an increase in costs necessary before the goods can be brought to market.

    e. specialization and division of labor between countries will be reduced.

16. Higher prices for imported oil have:

    a. increased U.S. incentives to find substitute sources of energy.

    b. reduced consumption of oil products since the quantity demanded is less at higher prices.

    c. reduced our balance of trade.

    d. encouraged the production of smaller cars in the U.S.

    e. all of the above.

17. A gold standard is one that:

    a. balances international payments through gold flows.

    b. sends gold to more nations that run balance-of-payments deficits.

    c. requires that all international transactions be paid for with gold.

d. ties a country's price level directly to the quantity of gold held.

e. none of the above.

18. When the U.S. was on the gold standard:

a. price levels were very stable.

b. devaluations occurred approximately every two years.

c. our balance-of-payments position was stronger than it now is.

d. it was easy for us to export our inflation.

e. our money supply was tied to the gold stock.

19. Tariffs can export unemployment:

a. if there is a strong labor movement.

b. only if the principles of comparative advantage do not work.

c. if you believe in the "infant industry" argument.

d. if they are only used for "essential" commodities.

e. temporarily, because eventually the protected industry will be forced to compete.

20. The exchange rate for the U.S. dollar will tend to rise when:

a. U.S. interest rates are higher than those in the rest of the world.

b. U.S. imports exceed U.S. exports for a long period of time.

c. U.S. inflation rates are relatively high.

d. there is a devaluation of the dollar.

e. U.S. investors are buying more foreign stocks and bonds than are being purchased in the U.S. by investors from abroad.

ANSWERS

Reviewing the Chapter

1. more
2. large
3. absolute and comparative
4. skis, shoes
5. 2, ¾
6. absolute and comparative
7. differs from, all resources are equally good at producing the two products
8. exports and imports
9. increased
10. exchange rate
11. price, depreciation
12. increase, more
13. lower, discourage
14. tariff, increase
15. increase, decrease, decrease, equality
16. into the production of some other good
17. are not
18. reduced
19. zero
20. increase, lowest

Self-Evaluation Exercises and Applications

1. Quotas:

   Without the quota, the price and quantity would be P_2 and Q_2. The domestic producer would be in favor of this quota because it reduces the supply of the competitive product and raises its prices, thus allowing additional output from the domestic form at higher prices than without the quota.

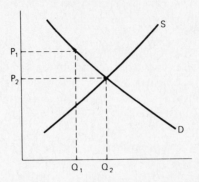

2. Contractionary monetary policy is favorable toward keeping the value of the U.S. dollar stable because it increases the demand for American dollars abroad. Foreign countries have been very unhappy about the deteriorating value of the dollars they have been holding and have tried to get rid of those dollars, thus increasing the supply of dollars and lowering their price. U.S. purchase of dollars abroad has the same effect: It increases the world price of the dollar. Tighter money in the U.S. tends to reduce inflation, making our products more competitive abroad, increasing our exports, making foreigners' products less desirable here, and reducing our imports. Tighter money is usually accompanied by higher interest rates, which will encourage capital to flow to the U.S. The improvement in the competitive position of the dollar was particularly apparent in 1981.

3. The oil-producing countries are accurate in their assessment of the role of our inflation on their oil prices. As the buying power of the American dollar falls, a given barrel of oil sold to the U.S. is being exchanged for less and less real product. The answer doesn't change if the oil-producing countries don't spend their money in the U.S.—they are still forced to exchange dollars for other currencies in order to use the money earned in the transaction.

Chapter Test

True/False Questions

1. false	4. false	7. true	10. true
2. true	5. false	8. true	
3. false	6. false	9. true	

Multiple-Choice Questions

1. c; 2. e; 3. c; 4. e; 5. a; 6. e; 7. d; 8. e; 9. e; 10. c; 11. e; 12. d; 13. c;
14. a; 15. d; 16. e; 17. a; 18. e; 19. e; 20. a.